The Metz

Book of Hackle

BOOKS BY ERIC LEISER

Fly-Tying Materials
The Caddis and the Angler (with Larry Solomon)
The Complete Book of Fly Tying
Stoneflies for the Angler (with Robert H. Boyle)
The Metz Book of Hackle

The Metz

Book of Hackle

Eric Leiser

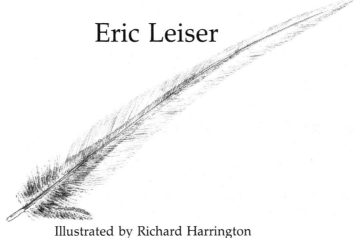

Illustrated by Richard Harrington

Photographs by
Matthew Vinciguerra

Nick Lyons Books

Printed in the United States of America

10 9 8 7 6 5 4 3 2 1

Library of Congress Cataloging-in-Publication Data

Leiser, Eric, 1929-
  The Metz book of hackle.

  "Nick Lyons books."
  1. Hackles (Fly tying) I. Title.
SH451.L4326 1986   799.1'2   86–24710
ISBN 0–8329–0424–4 (pbk.)

To June

Contents

The Metz
Book of Hackle

1

Hacklemania

What is hackle? To a fly tier the word *hackle* has many different meanings. It may refer to the specific neck feather that is wound around the hook shank to form the supportive collar on a dry fly, or to the soft webby fibers from a hen feather that are used as the throat on a streamer fly or the legs of a nymph. *Hackle* may be used to define a component part of the makeup of a specific fly pattern or it may refer to a material that is to be used in a particular pattern recipe. There is partridge hackle, guinea fowl hackle, hackle made from hair fibers, rubber hackle, and countless other materials, both natural and synthetic, that employ the term "hackle" to connote a function, a part of a fly, or a purpose.

For the most part, however, and for the purposes of this book, I am going to talk about the hackle feathers that form the plumage of the common chicken, particularly that one most-sought-after material in every fly tier's collection of feathers and furs, the rooster neck.

Fly tiers, like pack rats, collect anything and everything that might possibly be used to construct a fly. There is one item, however, that brings out the worst in the best of them and that is that ultimate prize—a rooster-hackle cape harboring feathers of the most elusive shades, the stiffest of fibers, and a full range of related hook sizes. It is easier to borrow a handcrafted cane rod from an angler than to beg a single feather from such a prized neck. Exceptional necks are seldom tied with. More often than not they are stored in containers liberally sprinkled with mothballs and are only taken out for viewing and inspection by trusted fly-tying friends. Bob Rifchin, editor of United Fly Tyers' *Roundtable*, is one such hoarder. He has suitcases of specially selected rooster necks, the hackles of which have never made it to a hook, much less a trout. If there ever was a pack-rat Rat Pack, Rifchin would be its leader, and he would have many followers.

Why this craze for the hackle cape or rooster neck? Is it because we need them for better than 90 percent of the flies we tie, or because no two are exactly alike and collecting them is such an enjoyable hobby? Whatever the reason, fly tiers today have a better chance than ever of finding the perfect neck. Until a relatively few years ago, this was not the case.

Prior to 1970 most of the hackle fly tiers used was from rooster necks and saddles imported from such Asian countries as India, China, and the Philippines. The common barnyard rooster in this country, though having fair-to-good quality hackle in some cases, simply does not produce feathers with the narrow fiber length required in most dry-fly patterns. The necks from India and other Far East countries, being of a more primitive strain, are smaller, not only in overall size, but especially in the length of the fiber, or barb, protruding from the center stem of the neck feather. Many of these chickens are direct descendants of wild birds such as the red, gray, and green jungle fowl, and this may be the reason for the quality of their hackles, most of which are stiff and resilient.

Hackles were also imported from supply houses in England but these were not necessarily of the old English gamecock strain, which were prized by British fly tiers for their stiff, web-free hackles. (English gamecocks were used primarily for pit fighting and only a portion of their plumage found its way to the fly tier's bench.) Many of the neck- and saddle-hackle feathers we purchased from the British Isles came by way of Asia or other countries.

Chickens are raised as food in just about every country and under most climatic conditions throughout the world. There are many breeds and variations, most of which are unsuitable for the smaller dry flies. Andalusia, a region in southwestern Spain, for example, is the home of the breed of Andalusian chicken from which the steel-blue-dun hackle color emerges that is so often sought after by fly tiers because it imitates the wings and legs of many of our natural insects. However, the purebred Andalusian cock has very soft and heavily webbed neck- and saddle-hackle feathers not suited for dry flies. Only the spade hackles, which are long, barbed, and of a beautiful speckled shade of dun spots on cream-to-ginger fibers are used, mostly for skaters and spiders. The Andalusian breed in Spain is a highly guarded strain and rarely, if ever, are the birds exported for further breeding with other strains, though this may have occurred in the distant past and contributed to other genetic strains of blue dun in this country.

Perhaps an illustrated glance at our subject is appropriate at this time so you'll know exactly what I'm talking about when I make reference to some of the parts that comprise a hackle.

The neck and back of a mature male chicken are covered with a unique type of feather most commonly called hackle. Because the barbs (most of us refer to barbs as fibers) growing from each side of the hackle stem are free, or nearly so, of a structure called barbules, they do not cling or adhere to one another as in other types of feathers. Because of this trait, which fly tiers refer to as *webbiness*, cock hackles have become the single most important material for tying dry flies as well as many other types of imitations. To say that hackle is indispensable to the fly tier is not an overstatement. Let's take a closer and more scientific look at the hackle.

Anatomy of a Hackle

1. **Calamus**: The hollow base of the rachis or shaft, which grows out from a pit or follicle in the skin, and which has no barbs.

2. **Rachis**: The shaft—a stiff quill-like stem that extends upward from the calamus and to which are attached the barbs, which fly tiers refer to as *fibers*.

3. **Barbs** (Rami): The hackle fibers themselves, which extend or grow out from opposite sides of the rachis, or shaft.

4. **Barbules**: Minute hooklike structures that grow out from the upper side of the barbs and that interlock with adjacent barbs to form a coherent membrane. When these are in abundance, fly tiers refer to the hackle as being webby. When very few barbules are present we refer to the hackle as being web-free.

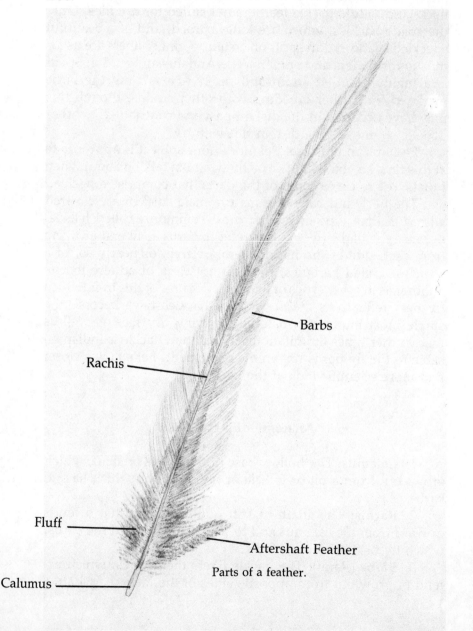

Parts of a feather.

5. **Fluff**: Sometimes called down—the softer, marabou-like fibers near the base of the feather.

6. **Aftershaft** or **Afterfeather**: A separate downy feather growing from the shaft just above the calamus and below the barbs.

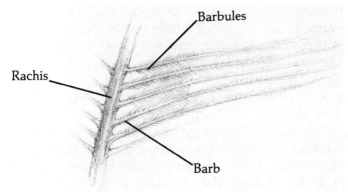

A magnified portion of Rachis (stem), barbs (fibers), and barbules.

Although much was available to us through importation and certain domestic stock, much was still desired. There was no consistency in hackle color or quality. In order to obtain a good imported neck fly tiers had to do a fair amount of looking and picking. But to a fly tier, poking through a carton or barrel of necks is like being a youngster turned loose in a candy factory. Most feather wrappers will sit there for hours if you let them and have enough necks for them to go through.

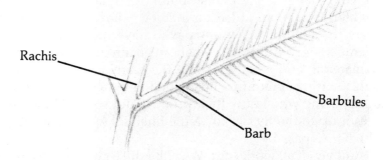

A further enlarged section showing how barbules grow from barbs.

The necks we obtain from India are collected by the exporter in that country from local butchers and farmers. They are then sorted into colors and degrees of quality by the exporter, who may or may not know exactly what is needed in a hackle feather to be used on a dry fly. Each of the Indian merchants has, I believe, his own ideas as to what constitutes a number 1, 2, or 3 grade. This fact has been borne out repeatedly over the years by those of us who have imported necks from various companies in Asia.

Each merchant in India has his own method of labeling. Some will call their best grade an "A" or "AA" while others will consider the "A" grade a second quality and label their best "Top Grade." I've even noticed one with a listing of "Super AA." It may just be that they are tying to outdo each other in their advertising in the same manner advertisers do in the United States. Unfortunately, they have not tried, as far as we know, to upgrade their product genetically through selective breeding and rearing methods.

When rooster necks are sold to distributors in the United States, the American companies are required to take an equal amount, and in some case twice that amount, of B-grade necks for each AA or Top-Grade neck purchased. This is demanded by the exporter so that he will not be stuck with an unwanted inventory of lesser-grade capes. Not so strangely, there are many necks in the B–grade category that qualify as Top Grade. But then, there is also the fact that not all Top Grade necks meet their labeled requirements.

When the rooster necks arrive in this country they are resorted by the importer/distributor for quality. This helps straighten things out at least a little bit. They are then sold to dealers throughout the country who have their own ideas of what makes for a number 1, what can go into the bin as second-rate material, and what goes into the barrel for a buck a shot. All this sorting, grading, and regrading by a number of individuals, some who know their product and some who do not, leaves it up to the fly tier to be the final judge of what is good and what to pass by.

And yet, it all works out. Why? Because no two individuals will select alike, or have the same tastes or needs, and it is the fly tier, after all is said and done, who enjoys poking through the barrel and deciding which neck will be used for his or her Ginger Quill or Adams.

In earlier days most fly tiers' needs went unfulfilled. Asian rooster necks, with rare exceptions, are not available in two of the most important shades a fly tier needs, namely, natural blue dun and grizzly. The dun color can be achieved by dyeing various light-colored necks into shades of gray. Dyeing, however, is always and only second best. Grizzly, as we know it and like it to be, is not raised in India, China, or the Philippines. You may occasionally see an Asian neck that approaches our barred Plymouth Rock in color, but generally the black-and-white barring will be ill-defined and the overall shade too light. Too bad, because the grizzly is the most important hackle of all.

If the chicken farmers in India, China, and the Philippines could have gotten together for the purpose of raising hackle for fly tying they could possibly have produced what may have been a superior neck by properly inbreeding the various strains. This will probably never happen. Asian chickens, as far as we know, are allowed to roam freely and are raised solely for food. You will always find many odd and strange colors in an Asian shipment of rooster necks because of indiscriminate breeding.

Still, there are some good things to be said about the birds in each country. Each has certain desirable characteristics we look for in fly tying. Chickens in India, China, and the Philippines are so different from each other that even an amateur, after looking over a few neck shipments, will be able to determine country of origin. It takes a closer and more experienced look to distinguish the characteristics of the hackle fibers in relation to fly tying.

Indian Necks. You can recognize an Indian neck by the cut of its skin. A neck skin from India is rectangular or square shaped. It is also much smaller compared to necks from other countries. Indian necks will have more small- and narrow-fibered feathers than those from China and the Philippines, and certain selected necks will have hackle fibers that are stiff enough to meet the standards for a high-floating dry fly. A top-grade neck from this region will be able to hackle a size 16 dry fly and occasionally a number 18. The only problem is that when the barbs on a feather finally get short enough to hackle the

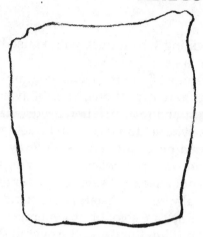

Cut of skin: Indian neck.

smaller-sized fly, the overall feather length is much too short to permit the required turns around the hook shank. Thus, an extra hackle or two is needed to complete the hackle collar. On very small flies an extra hackle stem adds just too much bulk.

Chinese Necks. The cut of the skin here is more rounded, almost pear-shaped, and the skin tissue itself is very thin. The Chinese are very precise and thorough and perform the operation of removing flesh and fat from a rooster neck skin very skillfully. Mandarin duck, which at one time was an allowable Chinese import, had a skin so thoroughly cleaned and scraped it appeared like heavy parchment paper with pimples. It was totally free of any fat residue, very unlike ducks from any other region. Indian and Philippine rooster necks, by comparison, have very thick skins, in some cases made even thicker by unscraped dried-out flesh and fat. This condition makes the necks brittle and one has to be careful when bending a rooster neck from these countries, for it may crack or break.

The hackles on a Chinese neck will fool you. At first glance they appear to be soft. When you pluck a feather to check the quality you'll wonder whether it is stiff enough to tie a dry fly. Surprisingly however, these hackles radiate easily and firmly around the hook shank and stand proudly erect. Chinese neck feathers have a finer center stem than those from India or the Philippines and this feature is what makes them appear to be soft. This fine stem is an advantage in that it allows for lighter-weight hackle collar while also reducing the percentage of hackles that have a tendency to lean or twist. Hackle size in a Chinese neck generally does not get much smaller than a size 14, though there is always that exceptional neck that will dress a number 16 or 18 hook.

The larger Chinese neck feathers with their wider outline and finer, more flexible stems make superb streamer and Woolly Worm hackle, far superior to those from Indian or Philippine cocks. Chinese neck and saddle feathers also have the best natural marking and color patterns, making them quite useful in imitating various smelt, shad, dace, sculpin, darter, chub, and stickleback minnows. They also dye well and make some of the best Matuka-type streamer wings.

Philippine Necks. Here the cut of the skin is pear-shaped, and the top of the skin, where the smaller hackles are, is very narrow. Most Philippine necks generally will not tie the smaller-sized dry flies, but for those who are tying variants, spiders, skaters, or salmon dry flies, these feathers are a boon. A few of these necks in assorted colors will provide a good supply of

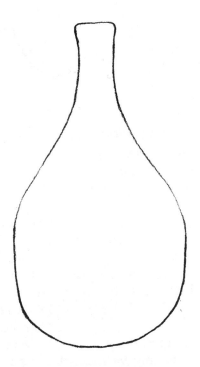

Cut of skin: Chinese neck.

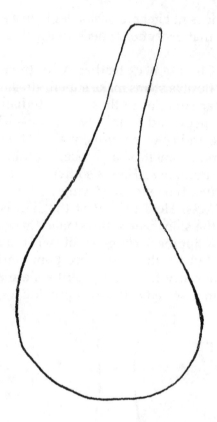

Cut of skin: Philippine neck.

tailing material. Philippine necks are usually inexpensive. The center stem is generally heavy and uneven in shape and in many cases will not wind around the hook shank without leaning.

As you can see, each of the imported necks has certain advantages. If you've been extremely lucky and your collection includes certain selected capes from each country, you can do a fair job of satisfying some of your fly-tying needs. But not all. You still need that grizzly hackle. You certainly want the benefit of the natural dun. And wouldn't it be pleasant to be able to hackle those size 20 and 22 hooks without cheating? Today, thanks to a handful of fly tiers-turned-geneticists, there is no problem in meeting 99 percent of your hackle requirements.

Genetic Necks

Until a few years ago no serious attempts were made to raise hackles on a large commercial basis solely for the fly tier. There was a small number of commercial fly dressers who, as a sideline, raised a few blue duns, gingers, and grizzlies in order to have on hand a better grade of hackle with which to tie their flies. The most notable of these were Walt Dette, Harry Darbee, and Bill Tobin. Andy Miner, who had a reputation for raising some of the finer blue duns, started his operation from four dozen eggs he obtained from Darbee in 1935. There were others, here and there, who dabbled in what has been termed "hackle herding." Incidentally, the hackle from those early birds was not necessarily obtained by killing the rooster and skinning out the neck. A good bird was plucked of a percentage of its neck feathers and then allowed to grow them back. But new-growth replacement of these feathers was slow and sometimes resulted in a feather of lesser quality until natural molt occurred.

During those early days of raising hackle for fly tying it was believed that a rooster had to be at least two years old before it could produce hackle stiff enough to collar a dry fly. Modern genetics has since disproved that theory. In fact, if a rooster gets too old he sometimes develops a heavier and possibly irregular-shaped center stem, which causes the hackles to twist or lean when they are wound around the hook's shank for a dry-fly collar.

The late 1960s and early 1970s saw a surge in fly fishing and fly tying. While there was a paucity of available literature on these subjects prior to this time, the decade beginning in 1968 more than made up for it. Suddenly there were more books not only about fly fishing and tying, but about insects, both aquatic and terrestrial. The most significant change these studies in hatch-matching caused was in the need for much smaller imitations of both surface and subsurface naturals.

Swisher and Richards, in *Selective Trout*, showed us that it was just as important, and in many instances more so, to imitate insects size 16 and smaller as it was to concentrate on the larger mayflies, caddisflies, and other insects, aquatic or terrestrial. Based on their findings and those of other angler/entomologists, our imitations had to be made proportionately smaller. Unfortunately, the hackle feathers from the imported Asian birds were not adequate for this purpose.

Materials, both natural and synthetic, and other specialized subjects grew out of this new wave of fly tying. Some were related, some specific, and some as far afield as John Betts raiding lingerie shops for fibers with which to tie his synthetic flies. There was an in-depth search for newer and better ways to make a trout fly and take a trout. As with all evolutions, revolutions, and resolutions, some things were good and some not so good. Some ideas stayed and some died. Certain new flies were the rage for a time and, like the old soldier, have since faded away, while others have remained to give us new and stronger options to cope with for today's fishing needs in both fresh and salt water.

One thing that did remain constant, however, was the need for more high-quality hackle. While Asian hackle had been good enough to get by with in the past, the modern-day fly tier had become too sophisticated to be satisfied. There were also many thousands more fly tiers than ever before and what little there was of the better-quality necks was being spread much too thin. In short, there were now enough knowledgeable fly tiers all over the world for someone to take a commercial interest in raising chickens for the purpose of supplying quality hackle to fly tiers.

In 1970, Henry Hoffman of Warrenton, Oregon began raising a hybrid grizzly that featured high-quality hackles capable of tying flies from a size 8 to a 26. It was an important beginning in a most important area because grizzly hackles are the most sought after as far as pattern recipes go. In addition to Hoffman, a few others also began raising birds with this plumage. In the East, Schlotter, Bittner, Brighetti, and Harder began producing exceptional birds of this type. The eggs of this hybrid were begged, bought, and bartered as each tried to improve his strain. Still, there was a lack. Hoffman and the other breeders only raised them on a limited basis and, for the most part, restricted their efforts to bantam barred Rocks and similarly barred black-and-white chickens. Some of these breeders are currently moving in expanding directions and striving for the duns, gingers, creams, and blacks.

It wasn't until Robert "Buck" Metz, Jr., of Belleville, Pennsylvania, a golfer turned fly fisherman, began to look into things in 1973 that true mass production of high-quality necks in all colors was started. Metz belongs to a family of poultry raisers and began breeding the birds as a hobby because he couldn't see spending good money for feathers from Herter's when there were so many chickens running around his farm.

He quickly learned that the commercial stock, mostly white Leghorns being raised for food and eggs, was almost useless for the requirements of fly tying. He purchased new stock wherever he could, including some of the Miner blue-dun strain. With the help of George Harvey, who taught him what to look for, Metz began breeding, weeding, and rebreeding. After many long hours, hard work, sweat, and patience, not to mention considerable investment, Metz achieved what no other hackle herder had been able to do.

Today he raises some sixty thousand or more birds each year for distribution all over the world. The Metz operation is one of the cleanest and most efficient of its kind and encompasses ten buildings, which include hatching, brood, and cage houses. All are temperature, humidity, and light controlled. The largest building is five hundred feet long—almost two football fields—by forty feet wide. Metz does not encourage visitors or give tours, especially to those who have been near or are associated with other poultry farms, for the threat of contamination from the outside is a real one. All the birds are checked on a regular basis—blood samples are taken periodically and they are injected against viruses and disease. Metz also splits his breeding stock into two or more separated groups to insure against any calamity destroying the entire stock.

When the birds reach maturity they are painlessly killed and brought to the skinning and cleaning room where a dozen workers, with surgical skill and precision, cape out the neck and saddle skins. Skins are washed, brushed, and pressed to a piece of special absorbent cardboard and then transferred to a preserving room where they hang from wires to dry for a week. They are then brushed, trimmed, and graded.

Metz and his wife, Sandy, do all the grading themselves, which is to the advantage of fly tiers everywhere because they are very critical and take exceptional pride in their product.

There are many necks they will not grade a number 1 but which would pass as such for most fly tiers. After grading, the necks are packaged and shipped to distributors all over the world. Incidentally, those necks that do not measure up are donated to youngsters or non-profit fly-tying organizations that offer free tying instructions.

In addition to Metz there are other raisers of genetic hackle. One such is Ted Hebert of Laingsburg, Michigan, who carries a fine line of blue dun and other types. That there will be others jumping on the band wagon I have no doubt. Only recently a company called Colorado Quality Hackle introduced a line of genetic necks in a fairly wide color range. Only time will tell if CQH can match Metz-quality standards. As far as I've been able to learn, it takes time and experimentation to develop *all* the requisites of a quality neck. Color is the easiest, but quality fiber length, stiffness, resiliency, and luster, while still maintaining color, depends on the luck of the cross and the persistency of the breeder. Metz and other breeders are constantly working on improving their hackle quality, size range, feather count, and color range.

Genetic necks are expensive. While imported Asian necks retail, on the average, anywhere from five dollars to eighteen dollars depending on grade and color, the retail price of the genetic neck begins at twenty-three dollars and retails at fifty dollars or more for a number 1. This is understandable when you consider that these birds have to be housed, fed, and cared for for a much longer period of time than are chickens raised for food. The housing and caging for these birds also adds to the overhead. Each bird has its own dorm with a food and water compartment so that it will not stick its head out between the wire mesh and bruise the expensive neck hackle it's wearing. There is also a more important reason for the caged isolation, and that is to keep the bird from pecking or fighting with other cocks or indiscriminately wandering into the wrong hen house and producing an unwanted color. Birds are only transferred into coed domiciles with specially segregated partners during the proper time. Special foods, diets, and medicines bring the cost up a bit more.

Metz, for one, does not kill his birds until they are about thirty-five weeks old, whereas a broiler or fryer reaches maturity in nine weeks. Also, there is a certain amount of loss in chickens that do not make the grade for fly tying. Being a hackle herder gets very expensive.

Regardless of expense, however, the question the fly tier must ask is: Is it work the price? Value is the name of the game when purchasing a genetic neck. Let's take a look at some of the advantages.

1. It is the only neck you will find in the color you want without having to resort to dyeing or bleaching (in most cases and for most patterns). The most prominent example is that of the natural blue dun. Natural dun is more insectlike in appearance because it is not a solid color but a broken pattern capable of reflecting light. Grizzly is another important color that cannot be obtained through importation, especially in the proper barring and correct hackle size.

2. Genetic necks provide a full range of hackle sizes.

3. You generally need only one feather from a genetic neck to wind a hackle collar on size 14 and smaller flies because the hackle, in addition to having short barbules, is long in overall length. With an imported hackle you often need two and sometimes three hackles to form the collar. With a genetic neck you will be getting twice as much usable hackle.

4. The quality is consistent. Simply because these necks are raised for fly tying, the accent is first and foremost on stiff, resilient dry-fly hackles. Of course, there are occasional throwbacks, but these hackles are not offered for sale. In the case of the Metz operation, hackle necks that don't make the lowest grade, a number 3, are given away to fly-tying schools, Trout Unlimited, and other organizations free of charge, for use as instructional hackles. United Fly Tyers of Boston, Massachusetts acts as distributor for these giveaway necks to schools and fly-fishing groups.

5. You don't have to spend top dollar for a very good genetic neck. Metz necks, for example, are also available in number 2 and number 3 grades. The hackle on these necks is, in most cases, just as good as that on a number 1. When hackles are produced genetically over a long period of time the quality of all the birds is improved. In fact, there is almost no really bad hackle. I've talked to quite a number of professional tiers, and most of them tie with the number 2 grade and some the

number 3 grade because they feel they get more for their money. The number 2 and number 3 grades may have fewer of the very small hackle sizes and there may be a bit more web at the stem base. On some others the tips of some of the feathers may be broken off, and even though the hackles are fully usable and of a number 1 quality, they are graded lower because of appearance.

You get what you pay for in the long run. In later chapters you'll see that by using both genetic and selectively purchased imported necks you'll be able to stretch your fly-tying dollar even further.

For those of you who want to know exactly what you're getting, I have selected three of the most-used colors in a Metz number 2 grade and had the feathers counted. Don Davis did all the counting. The tables speak for themselves.

Grizzly #2 Metz Neck

SIZE	HACKLE	BLOODS/SPADES	BROKEN
2	39	7	1
4	54	16	1
6	45	16	3
8	52	12	3
10	46	13	0
12	74	22	2
14	123	24	7
16	83	40	4
18	66	65	8
20	53	35	2
22	146	54	8
24	48	63	6
26	17	9	0
28	6	0	0
TOTAL	852	376	45

Brown #2 Metz Neck

Size	Hackle	Bloods/Spades	Broken
2	52	17	0
4	69	13	0
6	47	8	0
8	52	6	1
10	43	9	0
12	63	16	3
14	88	14	10
16	94	7	4
18	57	14	2
20	24	0	0
22	66	3	0
24	60	2	0
26	59	14	0
28	3	0	0
Totals	777	123	20

Blue Dun #2 Metz Neck

Size	Hackle	Bloods/Spades	Broken
2	20	12	2
4	64	15	4
6	48	15	3
8	55	9	2
10	43	7	1
12	44	7	4
14	92	15	4
16	66	30	3
18	70	48	8
20	75	55	4
22	63	65	10
24	55	14	9
26	10	36	0
28	2	0	0
Totals	707	328	54

2

Color and Quality

Rooster necks are available in a variety of shades ranging from white to black. They do not produce the brilliant hues found in some song birds. Colors like blue, red, green, orange, and bright yellow are not natural in chickens. Fortunately, any desired shade can be achieved by dyeing a white, cream, or any light-shaded neck into the color we want. In the photo-dyeing process even the browns and dark variants can be turned into duns. Bleaching is another process by which colors can be changed, though this method, no matter how carefully and expertly it is performed, does weaken hackle fibers.

Individuals see color in different ways. Each of us envisions a particular shade when someone mentions a particular color. For example, if I were to ask you to describe the color "brown," you might compare it to the shade of a chocolate bar, and if I then ask your friend, he may liken it to walnut. By the way, which chocolate bar did you have in mind? A Hershey chocolate bar is of a darker shade than a Nestle chocolate bar. And what kind of walnut is your friend referring to? Fly-tying colors have even more subtle variations of shade within their categories. A brown rooster neck, for instance, which is described as a red-dish brown in some catalogs, may be listed as a dark ginger in others; or, a dark ginger may be classified as a golden ginger in another publication.

Some of the confusion is caused by the roosters themselves because there is a natural variation and color overlap when the necks are graded into their specific categories. At times, it seems that no two rooster necks are alike, and in a sense this is true because they do not come off a production line like an automobile. Poultry raisers, such as Metz, will do everything that is genetically possible to produce certain colors and qualities, and in that it is almost, but not quite, a science. The neck you purchase is, after all is said and done, the product of a living, growing organism that has been hatched from an egg. This color uniqueness should be cherished because it gives us a far wider range with which to match the natural.

I will define the natural fly-tying colors for you as I know them to be. The color described will be what you see on the top, or outer, side of the rooster neck. The underside of all rooster feathers are of a lighter shade than that outer side that is exposed to the air. The outer side is also very shiny and lustrous, while the underside appears dull. When a hackle is wound as a dry-fly collar, the resulting shade of the collar is somewhere between the darker, lustrous outer side and the lighter, duller underside of the hackle. Some fly tiers, especially when examining duns, misjudge necks as being too dark when such is not the case at all. Always examine both sides of the hackle, then make your judgment.

White. White is the absence of other color. Now and again you will see a white neck with creamy overtones that cover part of the neck or some of the hackles. This off shade may be caused by an excessive protein diet or by a condition of being burned by manure. You'll find the latter more prominent with imported necks—it is rarely evident in controlled hygienic breeding. White necks are excellent candidates for dyeing, especially for some of the salmon-fly colors such as Silver Doctor blue.

Cream. This is an off-white neck with a yellowish eggshell cast to it. It is fine for such flies as the Cream Variant or a cream midge, but is a bit too light for the Light Cahill or the sulphurs, although some tiers prefer it for the latter two patterns. It is also used on such flies as the bivisibles and the Renegade pattern because pure white necks are fairly scarce. This color shows up very well when used as the front hackle on a bivisible. Cream necks also can be bleached to white and dyed to brighter colors very successfully. (If you put a cream neck in a bright blue dye bath the result will be a blue neck with a slight olive cast.)

Cream Ginger. This is a color category devised by me a number of years ago to distinguish the preferred shade of most tiers for tying the Light Cahill. It is a dark cream highlighted with a hint of yellow. It is not quite dark enough to be called a golden ginger. In the Metz genetic-neck series of colors you will find that the lightest of those listed as light ginger will fall into the cream ginger category.

Golden Ginger. Sometimes called light ginger or ginger, this neck has a rich golden or shiny buff color. The dictionary defines ginger as a yellowish or reddish brown, which makes sense when referring to light or dark ginger. You don't, however, see brown in a golden ginger. This color hackle is used in such patterns as the Ginger Quill and the Gray Fox Variant. In the Gray Fox Variant it is mixed with brown and grizzly to form the hackle collar.

Dark Ginger. A light reddish brown. It is so close to the natural brown shade that it is often sold for that color. As I mentioned earlier, there is a great tendency to overlap when grading or sorting and this tendency sometimes affects the listed ingredients in a pattern recipe. It's a good thing that trout can't read. Dark ginger is used in quite a number of patterns.

Brown. A medium-to-dark reddish brown, this shade is used in more patterns than any other with the possible exception of the grizzly hackle, with which it is often mixed to form a rusty dun effect. Fortunately, brown is the most common color available in hackle, whether genetic or imported.

Coachman Brown. A rich, dark, almost mahogany shade of brown. It is used in the Royal Coachman series of patterns but few others. This color is fairly uncommon in a quality neck. True shade is often attained by dyeing a brown neck to a darker shade.

Blue Dun. There is no blue in blue dun, at least not blue as you and I know it. The word *dun* means dark grayish brown. The term *blue* may have been derived from the blue Andalusian breed of chicken that was originally used for various "dun" hackles. A blue-dun neck can be a light, medium, or dark shade of gray. If it has brown or bronze overtones it is called a bronze dun. If it is so dark as to be almost black, it is called an iron dun. A pale watery dun is a very light (sometimes almost white) shade of gray. Dun hackles are used in quite a number of patterns, among which are the Hendrickson and the Quill Gordon.

Sandy Dun. This is a new shade of pale watery dun that was developed in the Metz hatchery. It has a pale dusky brown-gray shading and is very insectlike in appearance when wound as a hackle collar. It is used on the Pale Watery Dun and Pale Evening Dun patterns, among others.

Barred Sandy Dun. Similar to sandy dun but has an additional feature of barring across the hackle feather.

Chocolate Dun (Brown Dun). A dark brown neck with a definite gray overcast. This color has been naturally bred by Ted Hebert and Colorado Quality Hackle, and is currently being developed by the Metz Hatchery. It may also be obtained by photo-dyeing over a natural brown neck.

Black. As is. You can't have a light or dark black. You can, however, have a shiny black as opposed to a dull and lackluster black. Always select a black neck that is shiny and lustrous. It is used for tying ant and midge patterns.

Furnace. A brown or dark ginger hackle with a black stripe running down the center of the feather. The black stripe is actually the webby part of the hackle. Furnace is not listed in too many pattern dressings today but is used for the palmer rib in the popular Troth Elk Hair Caddis. (Actually, either brown or furnace may be used in that recipe.)

Coch-y-bondhu. A furnace hackle in which the tips of the fibers are also edged in black.

Badger. A cream or golden ginger hackle with a black stripe running down its center. Used in some caddis patterns, such as the Conover, and still very much in demand for the White Wulff.

Barred Ginger. This is a variant type of neck featuring a band of alternating colors of ginger and cream. If the overall shading is light this type of neck is often referred to as a ginger grizzly or ginger variant. In this case the hackle feather seems to consist of a cream color with a golden ginger barring. If the overall shading is dark, some tiers will refer to it as red variant or red grizzly. Here the hackle seems predominantly dark ginger to brown with a cream or golden ginger barring.

This type of hackle is rarely mentioned in pattern recipes yet is preferred by many tiers because of the color breakup, which more closely simulates the natural insect. A light barred ginger is an excellent choice for the Light Cahill pattern, while the dark barred ginger can be used instead of dark ginger in the Gray Fox and Gray Fox Variant.

Barred Cream. This is an off white with faint honey-dun barring. A product of the Metz hatchery, it produces a slightly more broken effect when tying the hackle collar.

Grizzly. A black neck with white barring. Perhaps the most popular of all because it is part of so many pattern recipes. Some of the most popular flies tied with this hackle include the Adams, March Brown, Gray Fox, Gray Fox Variant, Henryville Special, Mosquito, Hornberg, and countless caddis, streamer, and salmon-fly patterns. When mixed with brown the resulting effect is that of rusty dun. To the eye, many aquatic insects appear to be of a rusty-dun hue.

Chinchilla. A white hackle with black or dark gray barring. This color classification is not referred to very much these days. It has been replaced by and fallen into the general category of "variant." It is actually the opposite of a grizzly hackle and there are times when it can be used as a light-cast grizzly. Very few patterns call for its use. Still, it is one hackle I would not want to do without for the simple reason that it is so very dyeable. It will take to any color and the resulting effect will be solid with a fine barring—a nice breakup effect.

Barred Variant. This is the Metz classification for both chinchilla and offbeat grizzly hackles. Barred variants may be light or dark but the color arrangement does not fall into a recognized classification such as barred ginger or grizzly. The light-shaded barred necks are excellent candidates for the dye bath.

Cree. If you can imagine a grizzly hackle having dark ginger or brown barring in addition to the black and white you will have what is known as a cree, or as some fly tiers call it, an "Instant Adams" hackle. A true cree hackle should tie the Adams pattern without mixing in a solid brown or grizzly hackle. Most necks listed as cree are actually red or ginger variants with a touch of black somewhere in the fiber but not predominant enough to carry the effect after the hackle has been wound as a collar. Cree also lends itself for special effects when dyed in yellow, olive, dun, and brown dye baths.

Sandy Brown. A product of the Metz hatchery, this hackle features a white or pale-dun center stripe with the tips of the fibers also edged in white. It is a good choice for some of the tan caddis patterns because it adds a breakup effect.

White Splashed. A splashed neck is one in which the features are a bit mixed up. There may be some white feathers along with some dun-colored feathers, or sometimes the feathers themselves are half white and half gray. If you are tying Pale Watery Duns and Renegades this is a good neck because it contains both these colors. Incidentally, this is not a so-called "freak neck" but rather a purebreed that is used in a cross with others to obtain certain dun shades.

Freaks. (In the Metz classification freak necks are labeled as variants and include any neck with a mixed-up color arrangement.) Any neck with a mixed-up color arrangement. No one deliberately raises these necks. They just happen because of an occasional abundance of throwback genes. In imported necks they are a bit more frequent simply because roosters and hens roam about indiscriminately. Strangely enough, though they are not raised intentionally, they are in great demand by fly tiers and collectors. Everyone seems to want to have something different. Some unusual and effective patterns have been tied with them—the only trouble is that once the neck has been used up you can no longer duplicate the pattern.

Incidentally, don't be overly concerned with color. It is well to remember that all natural foods taken by fish, especially insects, minnows, crustaceans, and leeches, vary greatly in color and color pattern. Individuals within a species are as different from one another as are you and I. Many of these color variations are due to environment or physical conditions. You can meet many of your color needs by mixing your hackles—and other materials, for that matter. A combination of natural with natural, natural with dyed, or dyed with dyed can create some interesting effects. Size, action, and shape are equally important, or perhaps more so, than color in most cases. So handle the color problem as best as you can and don't let any lack of exactness annoy you. (See Chapter 4 for mixing of hackles.)

The saddle hackles of most roosters generally have the same markings and coloration as the neck hackles. Some exceptions would be the furnace or badger saddles on a rooster having a brown, ginger, or cream neck. For example, in the case of a rooster having true golden ginger neck hackles, the saddle's cape will occasionally feature the black center stripe in some or all of its hackles. Disparity in hen necks and hen saddles is another story.

Like most members of the bird family, female chickens are not as spectacularly endowed with colorful plumage as are males. The feathers are not as vivid or lustrous in sheen. The soft and subdued shading of hens, not only in chickens but in other birds as well, is nature's way of camouflaging and thus protecting the various species. Hen chickens also cannot "get their hackles up" like a rooster because the fibers of the hen's feathers cling to one another.

This webbing effect is caused by microscopic projections called *barbules*, which grow on one side of each barb. The barbules on one barb interlock with those of an adjacent barb. The hackles from a rooster are mostly devoid of these barbules except for the lower area, which we refer to as the webby portion. On the hens it is this barbule growth on each barb that gives the hackles a thicker and softer texture and thus allows them to absorb water more readily than can a cock's hackles. This, in turn, makes hen hackles ideally suited for wet flies, nymphs, and other subsurface patterns.

Many hen necks do not conform in color the way fly tiers want them to. A brown neck, for instance, is a little hard to come by because most brown hen necks tend to have the black furnace stripe running down the center of the hackle. Even the duns are a bit erratic. And, when it comes to hen-saddle patches, the feathers in this area more often than not are entirely different in shading and marking than are the feathers on the neck. Some of the markings on hen-saddle feathers are similar to partridge, grouse, and other finely barred birds. Wouldn't it be great if we could also find rooster necks having such speckled effects in brown and gray?

Yes, you can order hen necks or saddles in color categories of brown, gray, cream, or what have you, but don't be surprised if many of the colors you ordered don't run true. Few fly tiers complain when they get the offbeat shades. In fact, they are usually delighted with them.

Hackle Quality

When you go into a fly shop to purchase a rooster neck, what should you look for? The prerequisites are: color; stiffness of hackle; size of hackle; fullness of hackle cape, and tailing. Let's consider these qualities one by one.

Quality of Color. Obviously, the color you are going to select depends on which pattern you are going to tie. Whatever it is, you should choose a neck that has some sparkle or highlight in its color category. Light, whether from the sun or an incandescent lamp, should bounce from the neck being considered. Do not view any material under fluorescent lighting. It will only distort the color. A dull-looking rooster neck, while it may have very stiff fibers, is usually brittle. Dull fibers do not attract fish as much as shiny ones, and that is a very important consideration. Certain colored necks have more sheen to them than others. The browns, gingers, creams, and some blacks seem to glisten more than the duns and grizzlies. You should take this fact into consideration when making your selection. In other words, don't expect a dun or a grizzly neck to have as much luster or reflect as much light as some of the other colors. One other feature worth checking on a grizzly neck is the white barring that should be straight across the feather instead of being V-shaped. Give each neck its due and make comparisons only with categories.

Cock hackles that have been bleached or dyed should also retain their luster after either process. They should glisten and shine as much, and perhaps more, than natural colors. Color cold-dyeing techniques are usually superior to hot-dyeing methods because they do not alter the makeup of the fibers as much.

Stiffness of Hackle. We've heard some fly tiers claim that they've had hackles whose fibers were stiff enough to draw blood when they poked the tips of the barbs to nose or lips. The nose and lips are fairly sensitive and, supposedly, once you've practiced it a bit, you can check for stiffness of hackle using this method. André Puyans, of Walnut Creek, California, says, "The more it tickles, the stiffer the hackle." If you find this method works well for you, by all means use it. However, it is not really necessary.

When you have found a neck of the color you want, take it out of its protective bag (if it has one) and, while holding the tip (narrow end) of the neck between your right thumb and forefinger, bend the neck downward with your left hand and grasp the butt, or wide end, of it between the third and fourth fingers of your right hand. The neck is now bent in an arc and the feathers are protruding out and upward from the neck. With fingers of your left hand, brush or flip the feathers sideways and see how quickly they bounce back into their natural position. This procedure will quickly show how much life and resiliency are in the feathers of the neck. Generally, the more quickly they bounce back into position, the better the quality.

Brushing hackles with fingertips while neck is bent, to check for bounce and resiliency.

Isolating one hackle and checking for stiffness.

   While still holding the neck with the fingers of your right
hand, lift one of the feathers (use a popular size such as a 14
or 16) away from it neighbors on the neck and bend it in a
curve. Look at the fibers. Do they stand out erect from the
stem? Are they straight and not bent in a curve along with the
stem? Hold the feather up to the light. How far does the webby
part extend toward the tip? That part of the feather you will be
tying with—approximately the upper half—should be almost
free of web. Exceptions to this rule would be such hackle feathers as badger or furnace. The black center stripe in these categories *is* the web.
   If the fibers that grow out of the center stem of the hackle
feather are very stiff, they will support the fly on the water.
Occasionally you will see hackle fibers that are slightly bent
near the tip, or that have tiny feet instead of a pointed tip. This
is fine as long as the fiber itself, especially where it grows from
the stem, stands stiff and erect. Some of our most notable fly

tiers actually look for these tiny feet, claiming that they support the hackle on the water even better than fibers that taper to a point, or draw blood. Still others, just as firmly, insist that a dry-fly hackle fiber must be straight to support the fly high on the water.

Now and then you will come across certain necks that will fool you. A number of years ago I was examining an Indian rooster neck with an unusual dun color that appeared to be soft and good only for wet flies. When I checked the neck for bounce and resiliency, the feathers barely moved. They were limp and sluggish. I noticed, however, that the overall neck was fairly greasy. Greasiness in a neck, especially the imported variety, happens when rooster necks are piled or stored with the skin side of one against the feather side of another. With imported necks, the drying process takes longer because the skins are usually not properly cleaned in the first place. I purchased the neck anyway and upon arriving home washed it thoroughly in a mild dish detergent. After drying and pressing, I checked the neck again and found it to be of exceptional quality. Sometimes the extra effort pays off.

Something you cannot determine when buying a rooster neck is whether or not it contains hackles that are known as *twisters* or *leaners*. A twister is one in which the center stem of the hackle feather is not round enough to wind evenly around the hook shank. Hackle fibers on a twister will lie forward or backward and refuse to behave. Twisting generally occurs on imported or barnyard stock where the center stem is much thicker in diameter than in a specially raised bird. Don't worry about this aspect, however, because there are very few twisters. I've seen but one or two in all the years we've been tying. Most tiers think they have twisters when they really have what should be labeled as leaners. A leaning hackle is just that, it wants to lean backward or forward, just a little. This can be corrected, as you'll see in the next chapter. If you've accidentally acquired a neck having twister hackles, take it back to your supplier. In most cases, if you've not used too many of the feathers, the supplier will allow you to exchange it for another.

Size of Hackle. After you have inspected the neck for general quality you should check to see if it has a full range of hackle sizes. Lift a feather in each of several different areas on the neck and check the fiber length. The length of each fiber, or barb, determines the specific size hook it will accommodate. The standard formulas for determining hackle size on a dry fly are: Fiber length equals 1½ times hook gap; or, Fiber length equals ¾ of the shank length on a standard dry-fly hook. (See Chapter 4.)

If you're an average fly tier you will tie more dry flies in the size 14-to-16 range than you will other sizes. Are there an adequate number of feathers of this fiber length on the neck you intend to buy? Does it also have some of the larger, and smaller, fibered hackles to dress the March Browns and Green Drakes, or the Pale Morning Duns and the *Tricorythodes*? What you want to get is more of the sizes you will be using for your own flies. A good genetic neck, such as a Metz, carries a full range of sizes from 10 to 24. However, if you are only interested in tying the larger dries or salmon dry flies from sizes 2 to 8, you will do much better with some Metz saddle capes or some of the necks or saddles from India or the Philippines. Most fly tiers, however, will be tying somewhere in the 12-to-20 range and will be much better off with one of the genetic necks. You get what you pay for, and with this type of rooster you generally do not have to worry. But check them anyway.

Microphotography showing cross section of center stems of
a. Chinese rooster hackle   c. Metz rooster hackle
b. Indian rooster hackle   d. Philippine rooster hackle
Note slightly more rounded shapes in Metz and Chinese hackle.
(These are random samples taken from four necks. Stem configuration may vary from neck to neck.)

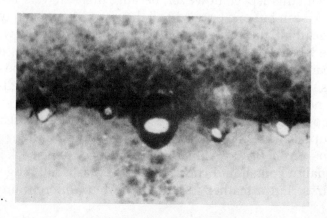

a.

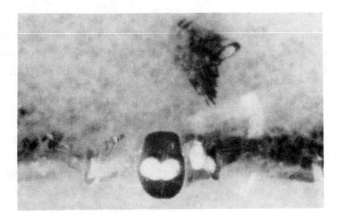

b.

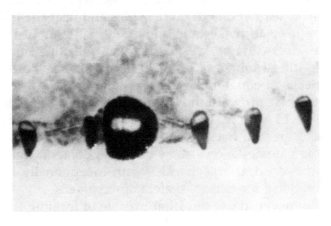

c.

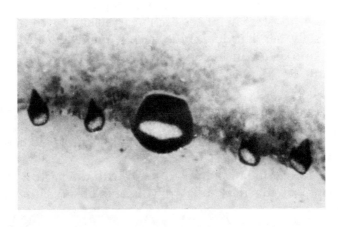

d.

Fullness of Neck. Some necks have more feathers than others. You won't have time to count the feathers but you can tell if you are getting your money's worth by how dense and puffy the neck is. If the neck swells out in a cushiony curve it has most of its plumage. But is it all usable? Look under the feathers and see how many smaller or half-grown feathers are present. This will determine if the neck has been allowed to reach its prime. A prime neck is one in which most of the hackle feathers have matured or reached their full length of growth. All necks have a small quantity of shorts, or undeveloped feathers, but they should be so few as to be barely noticeable. Of course, a number 3 neck may not have as many feathers as a number 1, but then, you won't be paying as much for it either.

Tailing. Some rooster necks have more than an adequate supply of feathers, both on the sides and near the butt, which can be used to make tails on size 10, 12, and 14 flies. Some rooster necks do not. Most of them have feathers for tailing the smaller flies from sizes 16 to 22. If you have a choice between two necks of equal quality always take the one with the most side feathers growing the longer hackle fibers. For larger flies, there never seems to be enough to go around. The side feathers are also used to hackle skaters and spiders. Incidentally, the very large domestic-cock show birds and domestic fighting cocks often have extra large hackles with exceptionally long fibers that are ideal for tailing, skaters, and spiders.

Try never to use a feather capable of forming the tail on a size 10 or 12 fly or smaller flies. In other words, don't waste a hackle having size 10 tailing on a size 16 fly.

Buck Metz, who with his wife Sandy grades tens of thousands of roosters he raises each year, has his own thoughts on how a fly tier can determine hackle quality. With his permission, and as a conclusion to my own thoughts, it is herewith reprinted.

How To Determine Quality Hackle
by Buck Metz

There are three steps in examining a neck to check for hackle quality.

1. Lay the neck in your hand with the narrow portion (nape) of the neck toward you and observe the overall

Buck and Sandy Metz, grading a neck.

appearance of the neck. The hackles down the center line
of the neck should lie relatively straight. The side or throat
hackles will usually have a slight curve to them. The neck
should be uniformly and thickly hackled with the hackles
being narrow and vibrant in appearance. The skin should
be flexible to aid in hackle selection and easy removal during tying. The overall appearance should be pleasing and
consistent.

2. Flex the neck at the point it begins to widen. This is the area that will contain hackles that are the most commonly used for trout flies. This flexing of the neck allows you to check specific size groups of hackle for quality. There should be a minimum of broken tips and stems. Only a few, if any, pin (incompletely developed) feathers should be present. Check to be sure the neck has a generous number of hackles in the desired tying range.

3. Select an individual feather for further examination. You need not pluck the feather off the neck, simply separate it from its companions. Check the web line to be sure there is not excessive webbiness in the useful portion of the hackle. Bend the hackle in an arc. The fibers should be short in relation to the length of the stem. The individual fibers should be stiff and uniform. Stiff, web-free fibers will stand out independently from the center stem and will spring back into position when flicked with your finger. The fibers should be dense and of uniform length along the useful length of the stem. Lastly, check the center stem for thickness and flexibility. A flexible stem will be a definite advantage in winding.

3
Storage and Protection of Hackle

As with all feathers and furs, rooster necks and saddle skins require a certain amount of care if they are to serve you well. If basic precautions are followed there is no reason why your hackle shouldn't last fifty or even a hundred years.

Rooster necks are particularly susceptible to three kinds of vermin: moths, mice, and beetles. Moth larvae, very small tannish worms, will attack the feathers, dissolving them into a pile of dust if the situation remains undetected for a period of time. The larvae of beetles, larger and fuzzy, enjoy nibbling away at the skin of your cape. A number of years ago I had the occasion to go through a newly arrived shipment of imported Indian rooster necks. When I opened the carton I found that the feathers on most of the necks had fallen out and were loosely scattered here and there. Even though the exporter had liberally sprinkled the shipment with mothballs, there were hide beetles everywhere. No, the exporter did not charge extra for the beetles. He wasn't, I'm sure, even aware of their presence. The eggs simply hatched in the warm cargo hold during the long sea voyage to the United States.

Mice will also gnaw away at the skins of necks, saddles,

or, for that matter, the hide or skin of any animal or bird. Sometimes they will even carry off the feathers and use them in the construction of their nests. Traps or poison can be set around the storage area to eliminate these pests but the best protection is to keep your prized necks in sealed chewproof containers.

After acquisition, all rooster necks and saddle skins should be carefully examined. This is especially true of imported types. Genetic necks, though they leave the farm on which they have been raised in the cleanest possible condition, become susceptible after arriving at a distribution area or supply shop because these establishments may have other materials in storage that may be infected. Most suppliers go to extra lengths to prevent any type of infestation, but as careful as they are, every now and then a culprit manages to escape detection. Generally speaking, you don't have to worry about genetic necks. Nevertheless, you should check each and every piece of material you bring home.

With rooster necks and saddle skins the hackles should be lifted from the skin and a check made around the base of the feathers for tiny balls of dust that appear as if someone had sprinkled pepper into the area. These peppery-looking balls of dust indicate that moth larvae have been at work. With your thumb and forefinger tug at the feathers in different areas on the neck. If they pull out easily check the skin side of that particular area to see if beetles have been doing any excavation work.

You cannot always see moth or beetle larvae, though you will, regrettably, see the results of their appetites. If you are the least bit suspicious, put the neck aside for decontamination. If you think the neck is vermin-free, but you don't want to take a chance, place it in an appropriately-sized glass jar and keep an eye on it. If any intruders are present they will, in the warm confines of your home, soon make themselves known.

Decontamination

If you have a problem, or suspect one, with any of your

necks, fill a dishpan with warm water, add half a cup of mild dish detergent (such as Ivory or Joy), and place the necks therein to soak for a while. Every now and again swish them back and forth so the soap gets into every nook and cranny. A nice bubble bath does wonders for both skin and hair. After half an hour or so (you can leave them in the bath overnight if you wish, and no harm will come to them) they can be removed, rinsed, and placed on newspaper to dry. When the feathers are almost dry, fluff them up by holding the neck by the tip, or narrow end, and beat them against the palm of your free hand. Fluffing the feathers prevents them from taking a set as they are drying. Replace the damp newspaper with dryer publications and let the necks air out some more. When the skin begins to curl, place the necks between more fresh newspaper, and put a few days' supply on top of the stack so that they flatten out and return to their original shape. All this changing of paper, fluffing, pressing, and repressing may seem bothersome but it really doesn't take all that long and the results will be a clean, presentable, and easy-to work-with rooster neck.

Storage

If you are convinced that the necks you own are clean and free of bugs, you will still need to protect them against future onslaughts. The best protection is prevention—that is, don't let any bugs near them in the first place. Necks should be stored in containers with lids that seal out moths, beetles, or any other type of insect or animal that may have designs on your hackle. I know of one fly tier who kept surplus materials in his garage. A handful of rooster necks he was sorting was left overnight. The next morning there were feathers scattered all about and the skin of some of the necks had been decimated. After a bit of fuming and a few expletives this tier set a number of mouse traps and eliminated the problem. He also never again left his prize necks unprotected. Household pets may be yet another problem. Most of them are meat eaters. The skin of your most expensive rooster neck is nothing more than that to your dog or cat—meat!

For purposes of storage I prefer large glass jars with a wide opening and a screw-on lid. The gallon-sized mayonnaise jars are ideal. Plastic jars are all right but you cannot peer inside them and tell what's going on. A few mothballs placed in each jar gives additional insurance. Incidentally, mothballs do not kill moths, they only deter them. Paradichlorobenzene crystals, on the other hand, will destroy moth larvae and act as a deterrent against beetles. It's always good to have a supply of both around.

Many fly shops put their necks in plastic bags when they are displayed for sale. Genetic necks almost always come in polyethylene bags. In addition to making for a presentable sales item, the poly bag, especially the zip-lock type, protects the neck against infestation. When you bring your necks home, however, they should be taken out of their plastic container and stored as I earlier recommended. Plastic bags prevent air circulation. If there is the remotest hint of moisture or dampness in a rooster neck and it is encased in a plastic bag, you will invite mildew, especially during the hot and humid days of summer.

Walt Dette, the famous Catskill fly tier, will tell you that rooster necks improve with age if they are exposed to air. Nevertheless, they should still be protected against vermin. Dette has constructed in the basement of his home a closet-type affair, the bottom of which is lined with Para crystals. His necks are hung by paper clips from rungs in the upper part of the closet. Dette claims that over a period of years the hackles actually get stiffer. This is due to the evaporation of some of the natural oils in the feather itself.

Once you have a vermin-free environment it takes little effort to keep it that way. Remember to keep your precious rooster necks in proper storage containers so nothing can get at them. When you acquire new materials, whether bought in a supply shop, harvested with a shotgun, or picked up as a road kill, don't forget to first isolate them, and/or wash them before placing them in the same containers with previously stored necks or materials. A hundred years from now your great-great-grandchildren will thank you for your efforts.

4

Getting the Most Out of Your Hackles

If a professional fly tier dresses a dozen dry flies an hour and sells them at a wholesale level of $7.50 a dozen, he will be earning an hourly wage of somewhere between $5 and $6. In order to earn more for his efforts he must: 1. find a way to tie each fly more efficiently so that he can complete more flies per hour without sacrificing quality; 2. cut his expenses by getting more mileage out of his hackle and other materials. Here are some of the tricks used by the innovative commercial fly tier.

Extending the Life of Quality Rooster Necks

High-quality necks are expensive. We can never seem to make them last long enough. Yet nearly every one of us has a collection of lesser-grade necks we rarely use. Why not, then, combine the two—that is, use the hackle from a number 1 neck with that from an old B-grade neck that has been lying around since you first began tying flies. For example, let's pretend you are tying an Adams, which calls for a collar of one brown and one grizzly hackle. There is generally an abundance of stiff brown hackle available simply because it is the most common color grown. A top-quality grizzly, however, is very expensive. If you use one hackle from a second- or third-grade genetic grizzly and one hackle from a good-quality brown neck you will have cut expenses without sacrificing the floating qualities of your fly. In most cases the quality of the lesser grades of genetic neck are as good as the top grade anyway.

Or, if you are tying a size 12 Royal Coachman, why waste two super-grade brown hackles when you can use one from your best brown neck and another from a number 2 dry-fly neck? It is even possible to find some excellent quality brown necks for sale at a dollar apiece simply because some fly-shop owners want to get rid of any oversupply in that color. There are also instances when many imported rooster necks are graded number 2 only because they do not contain hackle sizes smaller than a 12 or 14, even though the quality of the hackle may be superb.

Another example would be that of the Quill Gordon, which requires a hackle collar of medium-to-dark-blue dun. A Quill Gordon is usually tied in sizes 12 and 14 because these sizes most closely simulate the natural. When tying sizes 14 and larger it is always better to use two hackles instead of one because the winding of the second hackle not only fills in the empty spaces but also causes the first hackle to splay out just a bit, thus giving the fly better support when it is floated on the surface of the water. It is desirable to hackle the Quill Gordon with natural dun hackle fibers because they present a more lifelike impression than does a dyed hackle. Dyed hackles, however, are much less expensive because they usually come off imported necks that are used for dyeing. Why not compromise and use one natural dun hackle from a genetic neck and one dyed hackle from a grade 1 or 2 Indian neck? Using this combination will multiply the life of the size 12 and 14 hackles in the expensive natural dun by two.

Color Combinations—New Concepts

What else can be done with that more-than-adequate supply of rooster necks we've collected over the years? We purchased them either for their exceptional quality or, in many cases, because they were a shade we did not have. We'd like to use some of them, but somehow the various pattern-recipe books never seem to call for their use. There is another way out and that is by using color combinations to achieve a desired effect. Perhaps the best way to illustrate these combinations is to offer examples, using as models the fly patterns we are most familiar with and most likely to use astream.

Most of the imitations we fish with cover two basic categories: the dark flies, such as the Hendricksons, Gordons, March Browns, and the like that highlight the early season's fishing; and the light flies, such as the Light Cahill, Ginger Quill, and Cream Variant to mention just a few. The early-season flies, like the Hendrickson, call for a shade of dun hackle, especially medium blue dun or medium bronze dun. For some reason there never seems to be enough of the right shade of medium dun around, especially when every individual fly tier has his own idea of what medium blue, or bronze, dun should be. Usually the necks various fly tiers examine are too light or too dark. Why not, then, use one feather from a dark dun and one from a light dun to obtain the desired shade? That's actually closer to nature's way of color patterning live insects. Look at a mayfly wing or leg under a four-power magnification. A gray leg or wing suddenly becomes a patchwork spectrum of two, three, four, or more colors. You can even control the degree of color shading by the number of turns taken with either hackle. In other words, if you take an extra turn with the dark hackle, the fly will be just a shade darker, or an extra turn with the light hackle will make the fly appear lighter in overall color. If you wish to save a little more money using this process, use a dyed dark dun and a natural light dun for the process, or vice versa.

Some fly tiers prefer their Hendricksons with a bronze-cast hackle collar. Though there are some naturals available in this shade and the color can be achieved by dyeing, bronze dun seems to be a bit scarce. You can create your own bronze effect by mixing one dark ginger hackle with a medium dun.

A list follows of color combinations you can use to obtain certain results for both dark and light flies, and also various combinations for certain effects. They are not all the combinations available but I think that once you have begun to experiment with those listed you will discover more of them on your own. If you should come across any you feel I should know about, I wish you'd let me in on them. I'm always delighted to find new and usable hackle combinations.

Dark-Fly Color Combinations

1. 1 dark dun hackle + 1 light dun hackle = medium dun

2. 1 natural light dun hackle + 1 dyed dark dun hackle = medium dun

3. 1 medium dyed dun hackle + 1 grizzly hackle = medium speckled dun (The grizzly hackle will add natural breakup for a lifelike impression.)

4. 1 white hackle + 1 medium dun hackle = pale dun

5. 1 black hackle + 1 pale dun or 1 sandy dun hackle = medium dun

6. 1 black hackle + 1 medium dun hackle = dark dun

7. 1 medium dun hackle + 1 dark ginger hackle = medium bronze dun

8. 1 medium dun hackle + 1 dark barred-ginger hackle = medium bronze dun (Use of a variant-type hackle adds more breakup effect to the pattern.)

9. 1 dyed dun hackle + 1 dark ginger or 1 dark barred-ginger hackle = medium bronze dun

10. 1 medium dun hackle + 1 sandy brown hackle = medium bronze dun

11. 1 dark dun hackle + 1 dark ginger hackle = dark bronze dun (If deeper bronze is wanted, use a brown hackle with dark dun hackle.)

12. 1 sandy dun hackle + 1 sandy brown hackle = light bronze dun

13. 1 dyed dark dun hackle + 1 brown or dark-barred ginger hackle = dark bronze dun

14. 1 black hackle + 1 barred-ginger hackle = rusty dun (If possible, try to use a barred ginger with white and light brown barring. The effect is like the hackle collar on an Adams but a shade darker.)

15. 1 grizzly hackle + 1 brown hackle = rusty dun, as in the Adams (Light rusty dun or dark rusty dun shades are controlled by lighter and darker shades of grizzly and brown hackle.)

Light-Fly Color Combinations

Everyone has his own idea of what hackle color a Light Cahill should be. Some prefer an off white to cream, while others tie it using a golden ginger hackle. My own preference is somewhere in between. I've seen fly tiers go through box after box of rooster necks looking for just that right shade. The reason for this frantic activity is, of course, blamed on the trout. Whatever the reason, there is no excuse for you not to obtain the correct shade because if you don't find it, you can make it happen. The more necks you have ranging in various shades between white and ginger, the better the odds for the right, or desired, combination to occur. Here are some formulas for you to experiment with.

1. 1 white hackle + 1 golden ginger hackle = medium cream ginger (Again, subtleties of shading can be controlled by the number of turns of each hackle.)

2. 1 cream hackle + 1 light barred-ginger hackle = medium cream ginger

Anytime you can use a variant, whether barred ginger or barred cream, do use it. The additional breakup effect is desirable.

3. 1 cream hackle + 1 dyed yellow hackle = medium cream ginger with highlights (Some tiers prefer a yellow highlight without losing the natural creamy effect.)

4. 1 barred sandy dun + 1 dark cream = medium straw-cream ginger

5. 1 cream ginger + 1 dark ginger = golden ginger

6. 1 cream ginger + 1 dark barred ginger = golden ginger with breakup effect

7. 1 white hackle + 1 cream ginger hackle = cream

Most light shades for the Light Cahill or Cream Variant are obtained by using pure cream hackle, which is in plentiful supply. The same holds true for the darker light-colored flies such as the Ginger Quill because there is now a fair supply of golden ginger hackle available. Still, if there is any off shade you feel you need, you should have no trouble obtaining it.

Years ago, before the advent of genetic necks, the golden, or buff, ginger was a relatively scarce color, at least in quality. Those in the know simply mixed one dark ginger hackle with a cream hackle to obtain the desired effect. Today there is no problem obtaining this neck. However, if you want to extend the life of an expensive golden ginger neck, simply mix one Indian ginger variant with the golden ginger. It will also give you the advantage of color breakup.

Here are some random formulas that can be put to use as the occasion arises.

1. 1 badger hackle + 1 broken badger hackle = badger

A broken badger (and they sometimes have exceptionally good-quality hackle) is one in which the black center stripe does not extend all the way to the tip. Many of these necks are sold at a discount to move them. If you mix a broken badger with one in which the black stripe is constant, the discrepancy in the former will never be noticed.

2. 1 dark barred ginger hackle + 1 brown hackle = brown
Some professional tiers will not use this mix because it confuses their customers. Yet they will tie this combination for their own fishing because of the breakup effect.

3. 1 furnace hackle + 1 grizzly hackle = Adams blend (rusty dun)

There are very few patterns calling for furnace hackle. If you have an oversupply of these necks they can be used in your Adams pattern. The black stripe in the furnace hackle will blend with the black bars of the grizzly. The fly will be slightly darker overall but for some tiers this is a desired effect. A coch-y-bondhu hackle may also be used when mixing with grizzly.

When an artist is painting a landscape he has with him a palette containing many colors. Yet certain shades of nature elude him until he mixes some of his colors and transmits the proper hues to his canvas. You should strive for the same effect with your flies, whether to please your own eye or that of the trout.

Dyeing for Special Effects

The feathers of birds take readily to all types of dyes and the dyeing of hackles is not difficult. White, cream, and other light-colored necks are easily changed into red, green, yellow, and other standard shades. Dyes can be purchased from certain special-materials houses such as E. Veniard in Thornton Heath, England and E. Hille in Williamsport, Pennsylvania. The Veniard dyes, which include fluorescent shades, take a little getting used to because the English interpretation of insect colors differs from ours. They are excellent dyes once you become familiar with them. The Hille dyes are much easier to work with and they are fast and vivid in the bright shades and just about on the money in the offbeat hues of dun and imitation wood duck. Common household dyes, such as Rit or Tintex, found in most supermarkets will also do the job if you know how to use them. In some cases the supermarket dyes require a little experimentation. To obtain a bright red from a Rit brand dye, for example, you have to mix Scarlet Red with Cardinal Red (about half and half) to obtain the desired effect. Also, their standard Yellow won't quite do unless you add a bit of Golden Yellow to the dye bath. Whatever conventional dyeing you plan to do, you should always experiment first with several loose hackles or an inexpensive B-grade cape so that you don't waste a quality rooster neck. Be sure to completely rinse and dry your test-dyed feathers and check them in natural daylight or equivalent indoor lighting (do not judge under fluorescent light) to ascertain the color and intensity your dye bath has produced. Once you are satisfied with the color you can proceed with the dyeing of the entire neck. Also, be exceptionally careful not to overheat the dye bath or damage to the feather barb may result. Try never to exceed 170 degrees. Incidentally, the end result of any dyeing operation depends on the original color of the hackle. Pure white hackle will give you the true and pure shade for which the particular dye was intended. Off whites, creams, and gingers will change the end result to varying degrees depending upon the color of dye used. In some cases the difference is so slight that it doesn't matter, but in others you will have to adjust your formula. Both conventional dyeing and photo-dyeing methods are fully covered in my book *Fly Tying Materials* (New York: Nick Lyons Books, 1982).

The dye I like to use for special effects may be found in most drug stores, department stores, or beauty shops. It is Clairol's Nice 'n Easy brand of hair dyes, which are normally used to change drab brown blondes into glistening brunettes or turn back the hands of time for prematurely gray individuals. Feather fibers are, in essence, just like human hair fibers. Each package of Nice 'n Easy comes with a pair of ultrathin plastic gloves so you won't have to get your fly-tying fingers all smudged, and complete instructions that are foolproof. All you have to do is apply the solution to the feathers on a hackle cape as if you were dyeing your own hair. The only added suggestion I offer is that if you with to slow down the process, espeically in the case of dyeing to a very pale shade of dun, you wet down the neck feathers first. Normally, you'll get about ten to a dozen necks per bottle.

Bronze Dun. Dye required: Nice 'n Easy, Black. Cream, cream ginger, golden ginger, barred ginger, badger, and broken badger are the rooster necks that will produce the bronze dun shade. My own preference is broken badger or barred ginger because these necks are generally not listed in pattern descriptions. In other words, I'm trying to make use of those necks that are not too frequently called for but are fairly common.

The depth and shade of the original color of the neck will determine the end result. You will obtain bronze dun on all these necks but it will be more pronounced in some than in others. As you work the dye into the hackles with your fingertips you will see the feathers gradually begin to darken. When you reach the shade you want place the neck under running water to remove all excess dye and then wash it with the contents of the small container of conditioner that comes with each package of Nice 'n Easy. When your rooster neck has fully dried you'll want to make love to it rather than tie with it.

Necks always look darker when they are wet and you should take this into consideration when making your judgment for the desired shade. A quick method to determine the result is to pluck one feather, rinse it, and dry it under a hair dryer. This takes but a minute or two, and will tell you if it's time to halt the chemical action taking place on the neck.

Rusty Dun. Dye required: Nice 'n Easy, Black. For this color you will need either a sandy brown neck, which produces a true and brassy form of rusty dun, or a barred ginger that reflects the rusty dun through the reddish brown barring characteristic of this neck. Again, depth and shade will vary with the peculiarities of individual necks and the darker shades can be obtained by letting the solution work on the fibers for a longer period of time.

Speckled or Barred Blue Dun. Dye Required: Nice N' Easy, Blue Black. Barred variant, chinchilla, or light-cast grizzly are the required necks to obtain this shade. Do not use any light variant neck that has cream or ginger overtones because this will result in an olive or bronze cast. The barring of these necks is what gives the speckled effect after it has been wound around a hook shank for the hackle collar.

After they have been conditioned and rinsed in clear water the necks should be squeezed gently to rid them of excess water, then placed on newspaper to dry. The same procedures for drying necks that were described in Chapter 3 should be followed here.

Incidentally, Clairol makes quite a number of hair dyes in shades ranging from platinum blonde to black. They retail for about four dollars a package. Sound interesting?

NOTE: Birds raised abroad often suffer from a lack of protein in their diet. Because of this, you should darken imported necks more quickly than genetically-raised necks.

Sizing Hackle

Not all hackles run true to related hook sizes. Roosters simply do not grow standard 10, 12, 14, and 16 hackle sizes to correspond with the manufactured hooks of today. If you measured all the hackle in a given neck very carefully you'd find that in addition to the even sizes there are an equal number of odd sizes, such as 11, 13, 15, and 17. There are also some rooster feathers whose fibers on one side are longer than those coming off the other side of the center stem. This usually occurs in the hackles growing on the side of the neck skin. When measuring these fibers for a given hook size you should always measure the side with the longest fibers.

It does not matter that much whether you use a size 13 hackle on a number 14 hook, or a size 15 hackle for the same hook, as long as the overall proportions are adjusted. If the hackle is slightly smaller than a standard number 14, then the tail is tied in just a trifle longer. If the hackle is slightly oversized, the tail can be shortened to balance the effect. The important point is that the hackle tips and the tail support the fly in such a manner that the bottom part of the hook, just before the barb, barely touches, or rests just a hairline above, the surface of your tying table when you set the fly down. The height of the wing may also require a minute adjustment so that it blends in with the overall proportion of the fly, depending upon whether the hackle is oversized or undersized.

The general proportions for a dry fly on a standard hook are:

Wing—length of shank from eye to bend.
Tail—length of shank from eye to bend.
Body—length of shank from bend to wing.
Hackle—3/4 height of wing.

There are, of course, a number of devices on the market with which you can measure the hackle fiber for related hook size. Some of these, such as the Sturgis Hackle Gauge, measure the length of the barbs emanating from one side of the shaft or stem of the feather and indicate which hook size the particular hackle being measured is to be used for. Others may have you bend the hackle around a pin that is the center of a series of concentric circles relating the fiber length to proper hook size. If you think these are more useful than using the formula outlined in the previous paragraph, then by all means get one of them. Any time you can simplify the act of tying flies you should do so. After all, it's a hobby to be enjoyed, and the less complicated you can make it the more pleasure you'll derive from it.

Dry fly featuring recommended standard proportions.

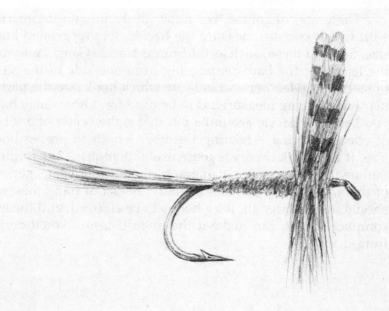

Dry fly with shorter hackle but longer tail to preserve balance.

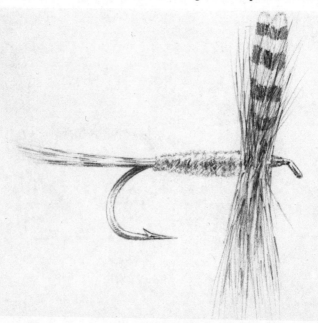

Dry fly with oversize hackle but shorter tail to preserve balance.

Whenever you're tying dry flies that require two or more hackles, always place the one having the longer fibers on the outside so that it is the first one to be wound around the shank as a collar. For example, if you are tying a size 14 Adams and you have a brown hackle that measures closer to a size 15 than a 14 and a grizzly hackle that measures a true 14, lash them to the hook shank with the brown hackle on the outside, facing you. The brown will be the *first* one wound forward to form the collar, the grizzly will follow as the second hackle. What happens is this: When you wind any hackle around the shank of a hook, you increase the diameter of the winding area. So, when the grizzly hackle is wound as the second hackle through the brown, it will have to travel not over the bare shank, but in between and also *over* the track of the previously wound brown hackle. Winding the larger-diameter hackle first will assure more evenly aligned tips on the finished fly. This procedure is to be used any time you use two or more hackles, whether they are of the same color or not.

Unless you have a keen eye, it is always a good idea to measure your hackles before tying them in as a collar. Walt Dette of Roscoe, New York, who has, along with his wife Winnie and his daughter Mary, been tying flies professionally for well over fifty years, still measures every hackle that goes into his flies.

Twisters and Leaners

You may occasionally come across a neck on which the hackles have a tendency to lean or twist. Though they are a nuisance to contend with, they can be made to behave by proper manipulation of your hackle pliers. They can also be made to behave with the assistance of another hackle. I'm sure that some of you have such necks and just won't tie with them because it is too much trouble. Why not give one more try, using the following suggestions.

A leaning hackle will either lie backward or forward. If its tendency is to lie forward, flip it over so that it will lean the other way. Take the leaning hackle and back it up with a hackle from a good neck, one you know does not lean and will wind very evenly. Wind the leaning hackle around the shank first. Wind the second, or good, hackle for one turn just behind the leaning hackle and corral the wayward fibers, making them stand erect, before proceeding through the first hackle to the tie-off area. The good hackle should support the fibers of the leaning hackle.

A leaning type hackle has been wound forward to form part of the dry-fly collar. Note rearward slant of hackle fibers behind wing. The second hackle, which has been selected from a neck without this trait, is ready to be wound through the first.

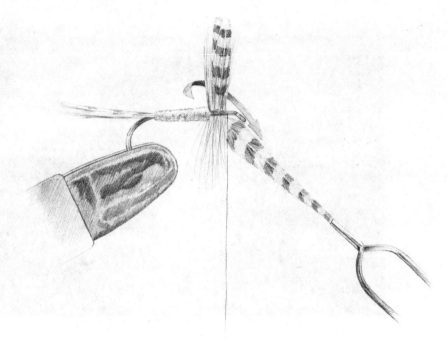

Second hackle has been swung forward, corraling wayward fibers of first hackle and making them stand erect. It is then brought around shank and wound through fibers of first hackle.

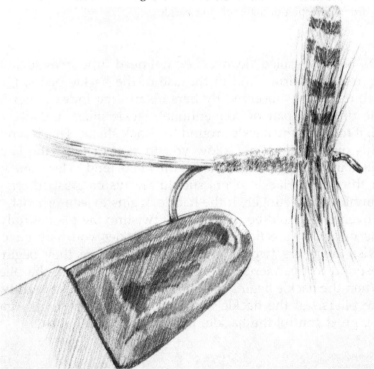

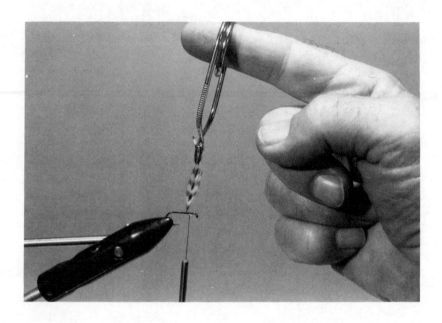

How *not* to wind hackle.
Note finger inside wound spring of hackle pliers. This method prevents
tier from correcting or manipulating hackle.

Some so-called "leaners" do not need support as such, but
do require a firm hand in the use of the hackle pliers. Quite
frequently I've observed fly tiers insert their index finger into
the ring of a pair of conventional hackle pliers and use this
digit to rotate the hackle around the hook shank. This is wrong.
This method does not allow you to cant or twist the hackle
pliers in an opposite direction if the fibers tend to lean one way
or the other. Hackle pliers should always be grasped *between*
thumb and forefinger. If the hackle begins to lean or twist, the
movement should be corrected by twisting the pliers firmly in
the opposite direction. With some hackles you may have to
twist the pliers two or more rotations before they begin to
respond to treatment. Do not, however, overtwist the pliers.
When the hackle begins to straighten you may have to untwist
the pliers lest the hackle twist in the other direction. Again,
you must control the hackle. Don't let it control you.

Saddle Hackles

Generally, when we speak of saddle hackles, we think of them in terms of wings for streamer flies. Saddle hackles, especially those from today's genetic necks, may also be used for dry flies. In most instances they are web-free for a much greater portion of the feather length and have exceptionally stiff fibers. Their only drawback is that they are rarely available in sizes smaller than a 12 or 14, though we have, now and then, come across that rare saddle hackle that will tie a size 16.

Saddle hackles are relatively inexpensive, even when they are raised genetically. By using saddle hackles wherever possible you will be able to spread your fly-tying dollar to include other necessary materials.

From left to right:

Spade hackle from shoulder of wing.

Spade hackle from upper saddle.

Neck hackle from side of neck.

Because saddle hackle is, as a rule, longer-fibered than neck hackle, it is a good bet for the larger flies, salmon flies, and variant-type flies like those introduced by Art Flick in his *Streamside Guide to Naturals and Their Imitations*. Variants, such as the Gray Fox Variant, Cream Variant, and Dun Variant, require oversized hackle. A size 12 Gray Fox Variant usually calls for a size 8 or even a size 6 hackle, and most saddle-hackle feathers will fill the bill.

Saddle-hackle feathers from imported necks, while also web-free and stiff, generally have heavy or uneven center stems that cause them to fall into the "twister" category. Saddle-hackle feathers from the specially bred genetic necks, however, do not seem to have this problem and in many cases wind even better than some neck hackles.

Saddle hackle is also available to the fly tier in loose or strung form. When it is strung, usually in China or India, the overall length is uniform and these feathers are used for streamer and bucktail patterns. Although they can be used for dry flies, most tiers feel that it's too much trouble to find the correct size in a bundle of mixed hackle; however, if budget is a problem, this is an inexpensive way to go as long as you don't mind sorting.

Some uses for saddle hackles:

1. Palmering Woolly Worms and Leeches (hen and cock)

2. Bass-bug tails, legs, and skirts (hen and cock)

3. Streamer flies and minnow bodies (hen and cock)

4. Palmering salmon and steelhead flies (cock only)

5. Legs or tentacles of squid flies (cock only)

6. Palmering saltwater shrimp flies (hen and cock)

7. Stripped quills for quill bodies, antennae, and setae or tails (hen and cock)

8. Trimmed and knotted quills for terrestrial imitations such as grasshoppers (hen and cock)

9. Variants and spiders (cock only)

10. Tailing for dry flies (cock only)

11. Hackles, tails, and wing cases of nymphs (hen and cock)

12. Hackles and tails of soft-hackle and wet steelhead flies (hen and cock)

13. Full-body palmering of wet bass and pike flies

Hackles for Hackle Tips

The Adams is the most prominent example of a fly using hackle tips for a wing. In this case it calls for the tips of a grizzly hackle. Years ago, when most of the grizzly hackle available came from barnyard roosters, the winging of the Adams was not too much of a problem because the feathers from the old barred Plymouth Rock were generally more rounded at the tip. The genetic strain of grizzly necks, while much better for tying a hackle collar of the proper size, is not quite good enough for hackle tips because the feathers taper to too much of a point. When used as hackle tips they appear too wispy, and though they are visible to us, it is doubtful if they make enough of a silhouette for the trout, and that is, after all, the point of having wings in the first place.

What to do about it? Take a closer look at some of the grizzly necks you have lying around. Poke your fingers under the overlying feathers and see if you can find some of the shorter, webbier, and not quite fully grown feathers under the canopy of prime hackle. For some reason, these shorter un-developed feathers, which most of us would discard, are perfect for hackle tips, and here is another example of putting to use a material that would normally be wasted. These undeveloped feathers are also found on other shades of rooster necks and have the makings for hackle-tip wings on such flies as the Pale Evening Dun, Sulphur Dun, and Blue-Winged Olive.

If you have to resort to the conventional feather on a grizzly neck for hackle tips, use the larger feathers nearer the butt of the neck. These are generally too large for making the hackle collar on the average trout fly, but will provide a better silhou-

ette than the smaller-sized hackle. You should never use the
hackle that is ideal for tying sizes 12 through 20 for hackle tips,
unless you have money to throw away.

Of course, as we shall see in the chapter on hen hackle,
the most prominent hackle tips are those formed by using hen
hackle or cut-wings made from hen hackle.

Hackles for Tailing

Because the tail on a standard dry fly should be as long as
the hook shank, there is sometimes a problem getting enough
tailing to support the larger-sized flies, such as the size 10 or
12 patterns. It should be remembered that the only portion of
a hackle fiber to be used for tailing is that part entirely free of
web. If even a small part of the webby section extends past the
hook bend, the tail will collapse and will not support the weight
of the hook. With this in mind we learn to be selective when
choosing our hackle fibers for tailing a specific size of fly.

In Chapter 2 I alluded to the fact that some tiers do not
discriminate when plucking hackle feathers from a neck for
tailing their flies. If you are tying a size 16 fly, you should not
use a feather with tailing that will accommodate a size 12 fly.
It is fairly easy to find tailing for a size 16 in other parts of the
neck because a number 16 does not require the extra length
needed in a number 12. Most necks have only a few feathers
with extra-long fibers to tie a number 10 or 12 fly. Always use
the longer fibers that are usually found on the lower side feathers for tailing the larger flies, and the center feathers that have
the shorter fibers for the smaller flies. Never waste a long-
fibered hackle on a small fly.

If, however, the necks you have are not blessed with enough
long-fibered feathers for tailing your larger patterns, you can
use spade hackle. Spade hackle comes from the upper back of
a saddle-hackle patch or the shoulders of the wings of a rooster.
Unfortunately, spade hackle from wing shoulders is not readily
available from supply houses because it is not profitable for a
hackle herder to pluck and package these feathers. The Metz
Hatchery does make available the spade hackle from the upper

back of the saddle. These hackles, which are still attached to a strip of skin, are sold under the name *saddle trimmings*. The fibers on these hackles are long enough for tailing the larger-sized patterns and in many cases are suitable for the tying of skaters and spiders. Spade hackles are short, squat, and almost triangular in shape, and although they do not contain as many barbs as a standard neck or saddle feather, the barbs they do have are usually long and stiff.

If you still cannot obtain enough tailing for your larger flies you can use what you have and compensate by tying a slightly larger than normal hackle collar. The same principle that was used for oversized hackle applies here. The larger-diameter hackle collar will angle the front part of the hook upward and allow the shortened tail to make contact with the surface of the water before the hook, thus keeping the fly afloat on an even keel. Incidentally, if you want a little better support for your fly when it rides the water's surface, tie in your tails so that the tips flare outward just a bit. This can be accomplished by pressing your thumb on top of the tail fibers where they are tied in, just before the bend of the hook. Most tiers prefer a neat, straight, and compact clump for the tail of their fly because it appears so precise. The clump effect, however, does not support a fly as well as those tails that are slightly flared.

Proper Winding of Dry-Fly Hackles

There are a number of different ways to tie in and wind the hackle to form a dry-fly collar. If the method you have been using works well for you and you are happy with the end results, don't change. For those of you who are not satisfied with your own technique or the end result, I offer the following procedure. It may just be the simplest and most logical sequence you can use to achieve a neat and supportive hackle collar.

1. Select the proper hackles for the related hook size and trim with a pair of scissors, rather than strip, those fibers from the lower portion of the hackle that are *not* to be used for the collar itself. Normally, most fly tiers will check the hackle feather to see where the webby portion ends and grasp those fibers below the web-free area between their thumb and forefinger and strip them away from the center stem. When these bare and smooth center stems are lashed to the hook shank they can be pulled out inadvertently while making the first turn with the hackle pliers. By cutting these fibers away, as close to the stem as possible, you will leave a tiny sawtooth edge of stubby ends that will catch in the thread and thus prevent the stem from being pulled out accidentally during the hackle-winding procedure.

2. For most hook sizes two hackles form a more supportive hackle collar than one. Take two hackles you have prepared and align them, one on top of the other. With the shiny side of the hackles facing you, hold them diagonally against the hook shank so that the trimmed butts angle downward from behind the wing toward the eye. Bring one turn of thread around the butts behind the wing. Make sure there is a small space of trimmed butt behind the thread so that when you make your first turn with the hackle pliers you won't accidentally trap a fiber under the stem. Take another turn of thread around the butts in back of the wing and two turns of thread around the butts in front of the wing.

Some tiers prefer to tie in their hackles so that the feathers are back to back or shiny side to shiny side, and flaring away from each other. The idea here is to have half of the fibers cup slightly forward and the other half rearward. If you interlock the fingers of both your hands and make the church steeple of your childhood, you'll have an idea of what happens. Winding the hackle in this manner forms a more stable platform than doing so in the conventional manner. If it works with the particular hackle you are using, by all means employ it. The reason it does not work at times is that one of the hackles may have a tendency to lean one way or the other, and facing them back to back will result in the second hackle binding down the fibers of the first. It's up to you to make these judgments concerning your particular hackle.

Hackle has been trimmed close to butt stems and excess cut away.

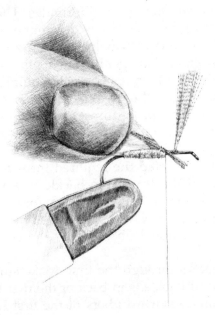

Hackles being tied to shank behind wing. Note free space of trimmed butts before fibers begin on hackle feather.

There are also those fly tiers who will tie their hackles to the shank with both dull sides facing so that all the fibers cup forward. This is not a bad idea for some of the caddis patterns that many anglers like to "pop" like a bass bug now and then to imitate the behavior of the adult caddisfly.

3. Grasp the nearest feather facing you with the tips of your hackle pliers and wind it away from you in a clockwise manner around the hook shank toward the eye of the hook, in connecting spirals. Generally speaking, you will need the following required turns of hackle in front and in back of the wing for each related hook size. This applies for each hackle: Size 12: three turns in back of wing, and three turns in front of wing, for a total of twelve turns for both hackles; Size 14: three turns in back of wing, and two turns in front of wing for a total of ten turns for both hackles; Size 16: two turns in front of wing, and two turns in back of wing for a total of eight turns for both hackles; Size 18: two turns in back of wing, and one turn in front of wing for a total of six turns for both hackles; Size 20 and smaller: Anywhere from three to five turns of hackle— enough to support the fly.

Again, the foregoing are only general formulas. There are times when the number of hackle turns is determined by the density of the hackle itself and the quality of stiffness of the fibers. Some hackles have less fibers per inch than others. Also, if you are fishing very turbulent waters you will require a more heavily hackled fly. If you want the fly to be tied sparsely you will have to ease up. For these procedures, and with much of fly tying, your own logic and common sense will show you the way.

4. When you have completed the required turns forward with the first hackle, hold the tip of the hackle in a vertical position and bring the thread over the center stem for two turns to secure it. Trim the excess. (Holding the hackle upright will allow you to get a few additional fibers under the shank for extra support.)

Wind the second hackle through the first. Make sure that the first turn of the second hackle is in back of the first hackle so that you can corral any wayward fibers of the first hackle. Rearward-leaning fibers of the first hackle can be scooped and propped up straight with a swinglike motion of the second

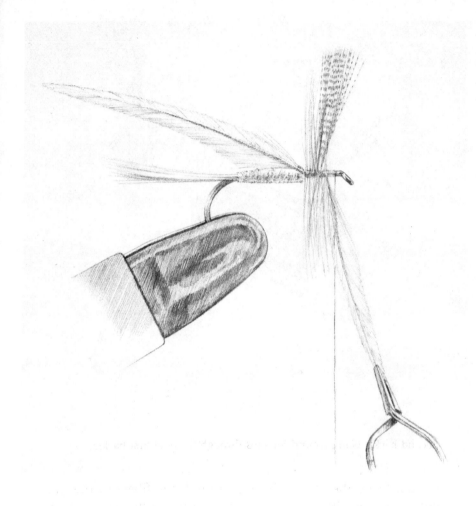

First hackle being wound forward.

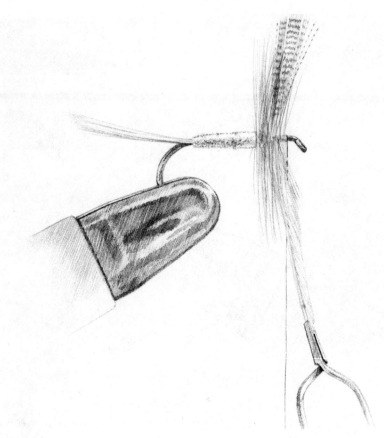

Second hackle being wound forward through fibers of first hackle.

hackle. Bring the second hackle through the fibers of the first imparting a slight back-and-forth motion to your hackle pliers so that the fibers of the second hackle settle comfortably between those previously wound. When the required turns have been completed, once again hold the hackle vertically by its tip and then tie it down and snip the excess.

If you should have a wayward fiber or two protruding awkwardly from the hackle collar, clamp onto it with your hackle pliers and pull. The hackle fiber will usually break off down by the center stem without leaving a stubby effect.

Fully described tying techniques for dressing complete flies may be found in my *Complete Book of Fly Tying*, illustrated by Dave Whitlock (New York: Alfred A. Knopf, 1978).

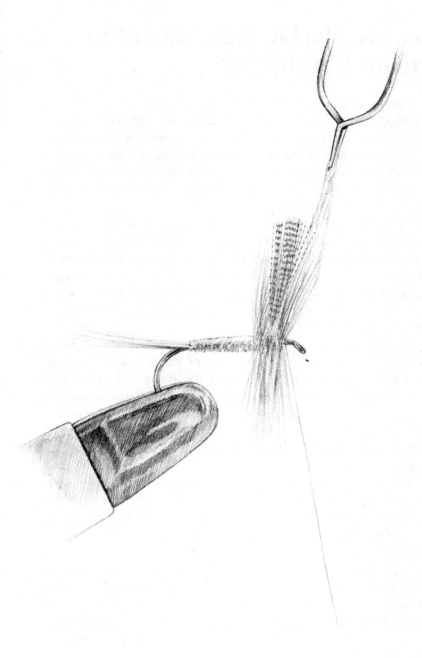

Excess hackle tip being held upright prior to tying down with thread and cutting excess tip.

Dry-Fly Hackle Adjustment to Stream Conditions

Understanding hackles and their various applications at the tying bench adds to our knowledge and improves our techniques when dressing a fly. However, unless you also know the attitude of the fly, how it positions itself in different types of water and how trout and other fish will react to your imitation, you will be unable to adjust to a given situation streamside.

Most fly tiers agree that it is necessary to use very stiff hackle for both tail and hackle collar in order to obtain desired water-surface position. It is also generally thought that the more barbs in contact with the water's surface, the higher the flotation and the better the fly fishes. Not so. A fully hackled fly is fine when used in fast or riffle-type water, but its appearance is unnatural under other conditions.

How the fly lands or strikes the water can achieve or defeat a proper float. If the hackles are out of balance with the body and the hook, if they are too long or too short, if they are bent out of proper position from casting, or are overdressed and matted with floatant or waterlogged, the fly will not perform as it should. Even the type of hook eye, the leader-tippet diameter, or the leader's flexibility may make or break the presentation.

The posture of a newly hatched dun, a dying mayfly spinner, a resting caddis, or a fluttering caddis are all different from one another. Because each presents its own unique silhouette, the arrangement of the hackles on an imitation must also be adjusted to that specific posture. For example, the mayfly dun rests on the water with only its six legs and a portion of its thorax and abdomen dimpling the surface. Thus, if you drop a standard Catskill-type dry fly next to the natural in smooth or pool-type water, it will not compare to the natural when viewed from above, and it certainly will not deceive a selective trout below.

Hackle barbs, or fibers, that penetrate the water's surface also cause an unnatural appearance as do the tail fibers and the hook bend. However, there must be a compromise in this less-than-perfect system of hatch matching and through it we will be able to fool most of the fish at least some of the time. The following suggestions should be of help.

When fishing a dry fly in slow or pooled water use as few turns of hackle for the collar and fibers for the tail as possible while still retaining flotation. As water conditions change from calm to slow moving, to windy, to riffling, and finally to fast

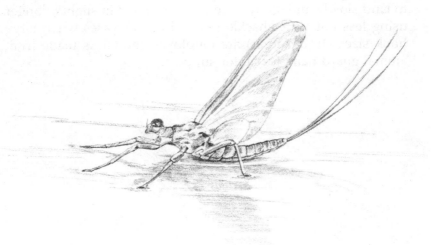

Natural mayfly on pool water.

and turbulent, add more turns of hackle for the collar and fibers for the tail as are needed to assure flotation. Happily, as we need more hackle the fish become harder pressed to see the imitation clearly because of distorted water conditions and have less time for inspection. The dry-fly fisherman trying to match the various floating aquatic and terrestrial insects must use fly designs from the no-hackle types all the way up to those using as many as four or five hackles wound as a collar.

There are times when fish want a very high- or very low-floating fly regardless of water conditions. The high-floating fly is usually designed with a very light wire hook to reduce weight, and is sparsely collared with hackle that measures from one and a half to two times the hook gap width. Higher floats are generally proportional to hook size, shank length, and wire diameter, in addition to hackle length and stiffness of barbs. These combinations also reduce weight and distribute the hackle over a greater area so the fly will have enough air resistance to land slowly and softly. The tail is also tied in slightly longer using less but stiffer hackle fibers. In some cases when large hook sizes (10 or larger) are employed the tail is made from animal guard hairs for better support.

Standard-type dry fly on pool water.

Thorax-type fly on pool water.

Natural mayfly on riffly water.

The low-profile float is generally accomplished by using a parachute-style construction or cutting away the hackle barbs beneath the body of the fly, as in thorax flies. We think you will be amazed at just how well parachutes or trimmed-hackle-collar flies float and elicit positive responses from fish. Hackle fibers that stick downward and penetrate the surface film give very little support and present an unnatural appearance in addition to causing the fly to soak up water and sink prematurely. George Harvey, perhaps one of the best anglers with the dry fly in the country, prefers to reduce the size of the hackle collar so that it is equal to the width of the hook gap rather than trim it. In other words, he is using a smaller hackle than normally used for a related hook size, and lowering the fly's profile and making the body and wings more visible to the fish.

For very low-floating insect imitations, such as spent may-flies and caddisflies, particularly of species in which the wings are thin and transparent, the hackle collar should be trimmed off the bottom and top of the fly. This design is far more durable and equally or more effective than the use of hen-hackle tips or cut-wing tied spent-style. Just choose a hackle feather (a grade 2 or 3 will serve as well as a number 1 for this type of construction) whose barbs are equal to the length and color of the spent insect's wings. Make just enough turns of hackle to suggest the width and density of the outstretched wings of the natural being imitated. If the imitation is to be fished in moderate-to-heavy water, make sure the body provides adequate buoyancy and leave a few more hackle fibers on each side of the fly. A dry fly, therefore, depending on the job it must do, must be properly hackled not only to float but also to make the desired impression on feeding fish.

To sum up some of the things I have been discussing in the preceeding pages, perhaps a quote from Dave Whitlock, something he has expressed many times in the past, is in order: "One of the most challenging and rewarding parts of fly fishing is the successful imitation of a live active surface or airborne insect the fish are rising to. No other material I know of more precisely performs this magic than the unique, stiff, shiny, transparent fibers of the mature cock-hackle feather. At rest, floating with the wind or current, twitched, or skated over the

Thorax-type fly on riffly water.

Standard-type dry fly on riffly water.

surface, fish seem to be completely convinced of the fly's faithfulness to the actual living insect it imitates."

And another quote from Dave:

"There is a silent confidence in the appearance of a fly tied with premium-quality hackle that stems from many lifetimes of experience and the success such flies offered our forefather anglers and contemporary teachers. Such confidence is the key to success to both newcomers and experts alike. The grand thing about these facts is that our supply of hackles has never been so good and continues to increase in quality and quantity, insuring nothing but better times for the fly tier and the fly fisher. We have also progressed to the point where we finally understand the true value of wild fish and natural foods and their importance to environment and welfare. The future will provide better fishing than most of us have experienced these last five or six decades."

Hackles for Wet Flies

When tying wet flies I recommend the use of hen hackle wherever possible. Hen hackle, which is almost all web, produces a sleazy, limp, and undulating effect that is exactly what you want when fishing. The fly should pulse and quiver beneath the surface of the water when the current moves it or when you strip or hand-retrieve it. Dry fly hackle, for the most part, is too stiff and will not move or pulse as well except in very swift water or when twitched more emphatically. However, if you don't have any hen hackle, here's a chance to use what may possibly be the worst grade of rooster necks you have hanging around. Try to find the softest, limpest hackle for tying your wet-fly patterns.

All hackle for a wet-fly collar should be tied in by the tip as a *folded hackle*. Each turn of hackle should be in front of the last as you wind toward the eye of the hook. Only the tip should be bound down by thread. The fibers that have made the previous turns for a hackle collar should radiate from the stem and slant rearward toward the bend. Fibers that will not lie in that direction when the turns are being made should be stroked

Hackle Folding Sequence

Hackle being held (shiny side up) between thumb and forefinger of right hand and third and fourth finger of left hand.

rearward and made to behave. Wayward hackle fibers are usually the result of an improperly folded hackle. When the proper amount of hackle turns have been made (about three to four on a size 12 hook) and the unused section is being secured by the thread, none of the wound-in fibers should be bound down by the thread.

The easiest way to fold a hackle is to hold the butt end between the third and fourth fingers of the left hand and the tip of the feather between the thumb and forefinger of the right hand. With the shiny side of the feather facing you, pull the feather between and through the closed thumb and forefinger of the left hand. If you apply too little pressure with the left thumb and finger the hackle will not fold. If you use too much pressure with the left thumb and finger you will strip the fibers from the feather. It takes but a little practice to adjust to the proper tension between left thumb and forefinger. For practice, use some of those lower-back rooster feathers you have accumulated over the years.

Hackle Stems for Quill Bodies

The shaft, or center stem, of the hackle feather can be used to rib the bodies of dry flies, wet flies, and nymphs. A good example of such use is the body of the Red Quill dry fly, made famous by the late Art Flick. In this case the center stem of a dark brown rooster feather is called for because this feather has the rust brown cast required for this particular imitation.

If these feathers are hand stripped of their barbs the pigmentation on the quill will also be removed and the desired color lost. The best method we know of to strip the quill and still retain the color is to immerse the quill, or a number of them, in a liquid bleach solution. When the barbs have dissolved the quill is removed and immediately rinsed in clear water or a solution of baking soda and water. This will stop further chemical action from taking place. Most fly tiers will prepare a number of quills, or use the lower half of a rooster neck and dip the entire section in the bleach bath, thus assuring themselves of a goodly supply for the future.

Left thumb and forefinger held directly over portion of hackle to be folded.

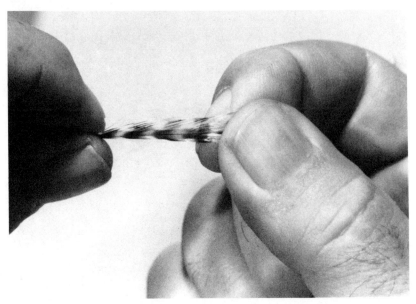

Hackle being pulled into and between closed thumb and forefinger of left hand.

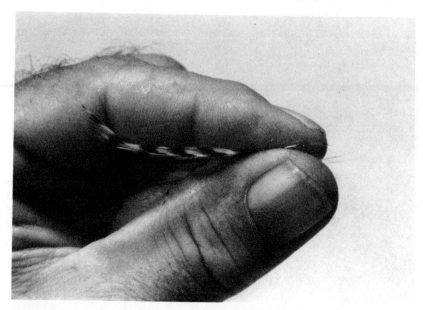

Hackle has been pulled between and to the rear of closed left thumb and forefinger.

Section of hackle feather that has its fibers folded.

Sometimes quills become dry and brittle, and if they are wound around the shank in this condition they will break or splinter. Soaking them in warm soapy water or glycerine and water an hour or so before the tying begins will soften them and make them pliable.

5
Hen Hackle

You wouldn't dream of fishing a dry fly with a hackle collar made from the feathers of a hen neck or saddle skin. The soft, supple fibers would collapse around the hook shank and the fly would sink. If you're fishing wet flies, however, that's exactly what you want the fly to do—collapse and sink. Hen hackle, unlike that of a rooster, will not stand proudly erect or maintain its shape. And that's just fine. Let it bend and weave and do its dance as it tumbles along with the current, vibrating and quivering and, at times, behaving much like a dislodged nymph or an ovipositing caddis struggling to reach the surface of the stream. Hen hackle was made to order for wet flies, nymphs, streamers, and all flies that are fished where trout do most of their feeding—beneath the surface of the water.

Very few materials impart more lifelike action than a wet-fly collar tied as a folded hackle using hen feathers. The technique of folding a hackle, as described in the previous chapter, applies to all types of feathers including grouse, partridge, pheasant, and even marabou. Hen hackles, however, are usually much shorter than rooster hackles and it may be difficult to grasp them properly to apply the technique of pulling them through your thumb and forefinger. If they are too short, clamp the tip of the feather between the jaws of a pair of hackle pliers. The hackle pliers replace the thumb and forefinger of your right hand.

Another method you can use when working with very short hackles is to first tie the tip, which has been separated and set apart from the lower hackles, to the hook shank, and while holding the feather vertically erect by the butt end, fold the fibers by stroking them rearward between wetted left thumb and forefinger. Be sure, however, that when you tie in the tip you do so with enough turns of thread so that it does not slip out.

There are certain feathers that resist the pressure of your thumb and forefinger, particularly those from game birds. The common chicken rarely refuses to succumb, though now and then you may come across a stubborn hackle in that family. If a hackle is giving you a hard time, moisten the pads of your left thumb and forefinger. This will sometimes turn the trick. If the hackle still refuses to be folded, don't worry about it. Tie it to the hook shank in the same position *as if it were folded* and as you wind it forward, stroke the fibers rearward and follow the principle of placing each turn in front of the other, working toward the eye. Marabou feathers are wound in this manner also, though here the problem is not getting the feather to fold. Marabou does that all by itself, flopping this way and that depending on which side is up.

Why all this fuss over the folded hackle? Because a properly folded hackle undulates more naturally than a hackle that has only been tied in and bound down with thread.

Another simple method of tying in throat hackle is the one devised by the late Charles DeFeo, who used the technique in the tying of his salmon wet flies. Simply cut the center stem of a hackle feather near the tip, leaving a V shaped section of fibers protruding from the end of the severed stem. Slip the wide end of the V of fibers onto the hook shank so that the tips point diagonally downward toward the point of the hook. Secure the fibers with a turn or two of thread and then slide the feather back until the desired length of throat collar is reached. Then secure firmly with more turns of thread.

A short hen hackle feather has been tied in by the tip.

Fibers are being stroked and folded rearward prior to winding hackle around shank. This procedure continues with each turn of hackle around the shank.

DeFeo Method of Preparing Throat Hackle

Hackle has had tip trimmed out and is placed over hook shank prior
to being tied down.

Hackle fibers have been secured to shank. Size is easily adjusted by
pulling back on feather, after which excess is trimmed.

Hen-Hackle Wings

Certain flies, such as the Blue-Winged Olive, Pale Evening Dun, and Adams, call for wings made from rooster-hackle points. Yet, if you have ever tied any of these patterns you'll have found that the rooster hackle tips on the completed fly are not very prominent. In many cases they almost seem to disappear into the fibers of the hackle collar as it is being wound around the shank in front and in back of the wing. Rooster hackle is generally too wispy—it has no body. On the other hand, if you use hackle tips from a hen neck, you will achieve much more definition. Hen hackle tips are also much easier to tie in and position on the hook shank itself. Because the webby fibers adhere to one another there are no wayward wisps protruding from the wing. It makes a neater appearance, is more prominent, and presents a visible silhouette to the trout.

Sometimes, however, it is difficult to find hen-hackle tips that have the proper dimensions for a specific size of fly, especially one of the smaller sizes. Yet the hen necks and saddles we have still have plenty of feathers on them. Why not, then, use some of these larger feathers and cut them to the shape of a wing in the size and dimensions required for the particular pattern?

Most fly shops and materials houses carry tools with which to make cut-wings. They are called *wing burners* or *wing formers*, depending on the process employed. The wing burners, such as the Renzetti or Iwamasa brand, are worked by inserting a feather between the mirrored wing-shaped ends of the device, pressing the ends together with thumb and forefinger, and holding a lighted match to the exposed material of the feather. You then burn away that excess portion of the feather that does not form part of the wing. This process does a reliable job but it leaves a charred edge on the wing that has to be rubbed off with your fingers.

Wing formers or wing cutters, such as those sold by E. Hille of Williamsport, Pennsylvania, feature a preshaped and curved cutter cemented in a block of wood. After positioning the feather under a base of a semihard but yielding foundation, such as pine wood or hard rubber, this tool is rocked and pressed over the feather, with something like a rocking-chair motion, thus cutting away the excess material and leaving a preshaped wing ready for mounting on the hook. This type of cutter needs sharpening from time to time.

One of the best wing-forming devices I have seen used is a homemade affair devised by Ed Shad of Paramus, New Jersey. Shad uses a clear precut rectangular plastic bar that measures 3 inches in length and 3/16 inch in height. The width of each bar varies according to corresponding hook size. The smallest is approximately 1/16 inch in width for a size 20, and the largest measures 5/16 inch for a number 10. Shad assembles these cutters by cementing half of a Gillette Blue Blade razor blade around the curved end of each bar. Crazy Glue or the equivalent is used for the bonding. (These razor blades split readily and it is suggested you cover the cutting edge with cloth when you bend them to break them apart.) Because the device is made from clear plastic, it is possible to see through the bar when centering a hackle feather before cutting out the wing. Shad prefers a foundation of basswood or soft pine upon which to do the cutting. When the blades become dull they are replaced.

There are those anglers, however, who are not enchanted with the cut-wing dry fly because the webby, solid wing planes cause the leader to twist erratically when the fly is being cast. There are those who consider the twisting of the leader a plus. One such is Art Broadie, of Peekskill, New York, who ties a Fan-Wing Royal Coachman in such a manner that when the cast is made the large breast feathers of the wing spiral in the breeze, twisting the leader. "Then," says Broadie, "when the fly lands on the water, the leader untwists, causing the fly to flip over. A few flip flops drive the trout crazy, and wham!" Nevertheless, most of us prefer a leader that behaves. Aerodynamics notwithstanding, cut-wings can be tied to reduce erratic flight patterns. Here is what you can do to alleviate the problem.

1. Position the wings of a cut-wing or fan-wing type of fly farther back along the hook shank, almost to the halfway point, much in the manner of thorax flies.

2. When the wings are being fastened to the shank, take counterturns of thread in a reverse figure eight between and

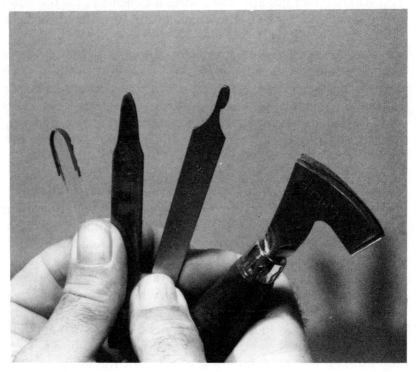

From left to right: Shad Wing Cutter
Renzetti-type Wing Burner
Iwamassa Wing Burner
Hille Wing Cutter

around each wing so they are positioned and locked in a slant-back posture as opposed to standing erect or leaning forward. This slant-back effect not only reduces air resistance but simulates the wing of a natural mayfly more closely.

3. When forming your cut-wings, place the edge of the cutting or burning tool close to the stem of the hen-hackle feather. In other words, keep the stem off center on each wing. You will need a right and a left wing for each fly. Tie the wing to the shank with the shorter edges facing forward toward the eye of the hook.

Are cut-wing flies really worth all this extra bother? Let's count the advantages: 1. the fly will land and position itself more naturally on the water; 2. it will have a more realistic silhouette; 3. you'll be able to see the fly more clearly, especially at dusk; and, 4. it is much more durable than a hackle-tip wing. In fact, all things being equal, you'll probably take more fish with it.

There is yet another advantage in using hen hackle over rooster-hackle tips, or for that matter, over some of the other materials such as wood duck, duck quills, and various hair fibers, and that is the variety of markings and color found in the neck and saddle feathers of the hen chicken. The subtle barring and shading found in these feathers resemble similar markings found on many of our natural aquatic insects. Except for black, it seems that each and every hen saddle is different from every other. In order to obtain some of these off shades you will have to go to a dealer in genetic necks, such as Metz, who carries the neck and saddle patches of these birds.

Mottled hen feathers are also used for the wings on caddisflies and for wing pads on nymphs. When you consider the scarcity and the current price of mottled-turkey-wing quills, hen hackle gets better looking all the time. There are, incidentally, Renzetti-brand wing burners manufactured specifically for the forming of caddisfly wings.

George Harvey, a former teacher of angling and fly tying at Penn State University and author of *Techniques of Trout Fishing and Fly Tying*, has found yet another use for hen hackles in the forming of wings on dry and wet flies.

A number of seasons ago Harvey was in the Metz Hatchery watching workers cape out the genetic stock. "Some hen-saddle patches were on the drying boards," he says, "and I immedi-

Two samples of cut wings: Left is center cut . . . may twist when cast;
right is cut close to stem edge and will perform better.

Properly trimmed cut wing positioned on hook shank.
Note rearward slant of wing.

ately acquired some for experimental purposes. I took the saddle patches home and tied up some dry flies using a clump of
hen-hackle fibers for wings on commercial patterns. The results
were phenomenal. The fibers from light ginger hen-saddle
patches were far superior for dry and wet Cahill patterns and
one could see the fly much better than the wood-duck-winged
Cahills. I have never been one," continues Harvey, "to put in
print anything until I was absolutely sure of its worth. . . . I
am convinced that this winging material is the best on the
market today. Not only will they look great, but once they are
dressed with floatant they will float indefinitely." Harvey uses
hen-saddle hackles in the following natural colors: white, brown,
light and dark speckled ginger, various shades of speckled brown,
light ginger, light blue dun, blue dun, dark blue dun, black,
and grizzly.

He is now experimenting with white hen-saddle hackles
dyed into shades of fluorescent light green, light orange, yellow, pink, and red for down-wings on caddis, deer-hair ants
and beetles, and regular divided wings on other patterns because of the visibility factor. "Flies tied with fluorescent wings
can be seen under almost any condition," he says.

The technique of using hen-hackle fibers is the same as
that used for wood-duck fibers. A section is cut from the feather,
fastened to the hook shank, and divided with thread. Because
of the density caused by the webby fibers the wing has more
opacity, thus creating a solid silhouette to the trout. The fibers
are also more durable and can easily be reshaped into wing
form after a number of fish have been taken.

As you can see, hen hackle has an important place in modern fly-tying theory. And I suspect that more space will be
allotted to its storage in the ever-expanding corner set aside for
fly-tying materials.

What follows is a summarized list of some uses for hen
hackles:

1. Wings for adult caddis, mayfly emergers, cut-wings, and
   spinners

2. Nymph legs and tails

3. Soft-hackle collars and tails

Harvey Method of Winging Flies With Hen Fibers

Mottled tan/brown hen fibers have been aligned prior to cutting
section for wing.

Completed dry fly featuring divided clump of hen hackle wings. Note density of fibers.

NOTE: The pattern used here is George Harvey's Spruce Creek Fly. The original pattern calls for woodduck flank fibers but Harvey now also ties it using mottled tan/brown hen saddle fibers.

4. Sculpin minnow pectoral fins

5. Wet-fly hackle, tails, and wings

6. Legs, tails, and other appendages for shrimp and crustaceans

7. Wings for moths

8. Streamer cheeks

9. Backs and shells for terrestrials (usually enameled)

10. Spider legs

6
Odds and Ends

I doubt there are fly tiers who, when they sit down at their tying bench, don't let their thoughts wander and roam in search of newer, different, or better ways to dress a pattern or to create a new fly. As enjoyable as fly tying is, you can only tie so many Adamses, Cahills, or Henryville Specials before the routine becomes monotonous. New concepts in fly tying are born out of boredom or manufactured out of necessity. If we're out of a called-for material we scrounge around and find a substitute that, who knows, may improve on the original pattern or lead to a desirable twist while fishing. All of us like to go off the beaten path and experiment with materials we have been collecting. When a brand-new material comes on the market it is an open invitation to innovation and creation.

I'd like to share with you a handful of flies I have been toying with. They have not, as yet, been fished with long enough to warrant a "Hey! Look at this. It's a winner!" but they have taken fish and with your help in field testing, perhaps one day you will see them in the pages of your latest tackle catalog. Each of the following flies features the use of hackle in one form or another.

Sandy Brown Caddis (sizes 12–18)
Hook: Mustad 94840, Partridge L3A
Thread: olive
Tail: none
Body: tan, gray, or olive dubbing fur
Wing: hackle fibers from a sandy brown rooster neck
Hackle: sandy brown

There is nothing unusual about the construction of this adult caddis imitation. It follows standard fly-tying procedures of forming a dubbed-fur body, tying in a down-wing wing, and winding the hackle for a dry-fly collar. What is different about it is the use of the new genetic hackle, Sandy Brown, which features a dark ginger hackle wing terminating in a very pale gray or white tip, and hackle collar that is also dark ginger but has a pale gray center web and a pale gray tip. It imitates a variety of natural caddis that have the tan wing and tan-to-light-ginger legs. The body color is changed to accommodate different species of caddis. This fly has produced fairly consistently when this type of caddis has made its appearance.

Featherduster, Bass (sizes 2–10)
Hook: Mustad 9672, 9671
Thread: black, brown, or gray
Tail: 2 grizzly hen-hackle tips
Underbody: fine lead wire wound length of shank
Body: grizzly hen-saddle fluff hackle
Head: black

The Featherduster series of flies features the folded hackle wound the full length of the hook shank. This particular pattern is designed for bass and uses the lower fluffy portion of hen-saddle feathers. If you check out a few hen-saddle skins you will find certain feathers that do not end up, or do so just barely, in a pronounced hackle tip. They are made up of soft fluffy fibers, not unlike marabou in texture, yet much shorter in fiber length. The action of these fluffy fibers is similar to that of marabou. They pulse, quiver, and breathe when being retrieved. The Featherduster has caught bass on a regular basis and I suspect it will also take its share of trout. The fly is

Sandy Brown Caddis

weighted because even though hen hackle sinks quite readily, there is such an abundance of it on this particular fly that it takes a while to disperse the air bubbles within the fluffy hackle. It is suggested you soak the fly in water before making your first cast. This pattern simulates both terrestrial and aquatic creatures swimming near the shoreline. It resembles mice, tadpoles, sculpins, or whatever a bass might take it to be.

The following sequences should assist you in the tying of this simple pattern.

1. Clamp a size 6 hook in your vise and wind a foundation of thread in close spirals beginning behind the eye to the bend of the hook.

2. Select two well-marked grizzly hen-neck or saddle feathers and tie them in for a tail with the tips flaring away from each other. They should protrude beyond the bend for approximately 3/4 inch.

3. Spread a liberal amount of head lacquer on the thread foundation and then build an underbody of fine lead wire from just forward of the bend to a point 1/16 inch before the eye. Add more cement to the lead wire underbody and crisscross the lead spirals with thread. Build a natural taper of thread at both ends of the lead underbody.

4. Select one of the fluffy hen-hackle feathers and tie it to the shank at the bend by its tip. If you cannot find a fluffy feather, simply use those that have the fluffiest base and tie on to the shank where the fluff begins. You do not have to fold this hackle—a brief stroking with thumb and forefinger in a downward manner will program it. The natural curve of these feathers on the "up" or shiny side, is downward. Stroke them in the direction they want to go. Tie them to the shank so that the shiny or "up" side is facing you. Bring the thread forward along the hook shank for 1/4 inch.

5. Wind the hackle, as far as it will go and before you run into the heavy portion of the stem, as a folded hackle. That is, with every turn you make toward the eye, stroke the fibers rearward and make each turn forward of the previous one. When you have used what you can on this particular hackle, secure it with thread, snip the excess, and select another fluffy hackle and continue building the body. It takes approximately three to four of the fluffy hen feathers to fill the hook shank.

Bass Featherduster

Grizzly hen hackles have been tied in for tail.

Hook shank has been wound with lead wire.

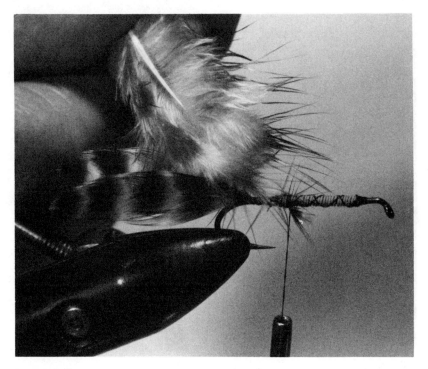

A soft fluffy hen hackle being tied in by the tip.

Fibers being stroked rearward while feather is being wound around shank, one turn in front of the other.

Completed Bass Featherduster. This fly required the use of four of the fluffy grizzly hen feathers.

The amount of hackle used depends on the size of the hook.

6. When you have formed the body with fluff to the eye of the hook, snip all excess and whip finish the head.

Featherdusters for bass can be made in a variety of shades. Some of my favorite colors, in addition to the grizzly, are black, speckled brown, and speckled gray.

Featherduster, Salmon (sizes 4–10)
Hook: Mustad 36890, Partridge, single salmon
Thread: black
Tail: golden pheasant tippets
Body: double-folded saddle hackle, one grizzly, one hot orange
head: black

Once you've tied a few Salmon Featherdusters you'll never forget how to fold a hackle. This pattern employs not one, but two folded hackles, one inside the other. Here's how to proceed.

1. Place a size 6 hook in your vise and spiral your thread onto the shank beginning just before and winding to the bend.

2. Tie in a few golden-pheasant-tippet fibers to form the tail. The tail should extend approximately 1/4 inch beyond the bend.

3. Select one grizzly and one dyed hot orange saddle-hackle feather. They should be as long as possible for a given hook size. The idea is to cover the shank without adding more hackle. Fiber length on these hackles should also be in proportion to a given hook size, in this case a number 6.

4. Fold the entire length of one of the saddle feathers so that all the fibers are in the downward set. Now do the same with the other saddle feather. Slip the orange saddle hackle inside the fold of the grizzly hackle.

5. The double-folded hackles are tied to the shank as a unit, by their tips. You'll have to make an open area between the fibers by separating them near the tip. Try to be precise so that there is no overlap of the fibers of one hackle with those of the other. Bring your thread forward, binding down the tip portion as you do so, and let the thread hang from the shank 1/8 inch before the hook eye.

Salmon Featherduster

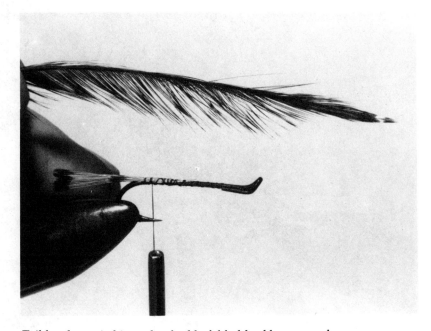

Tail has been tied in and a double folded hackle prepared.

Double folded hackle has been tied in by tip and is being wound forward, one turn in front of another.

Completed Salmon Featherduster.

6. Grasp the unit of double-folded hackle by the butts and hold it erect. Check to make sure there is no slack in either hackle and that they both are straight and taut from the hook shank to your fingers. Now begin winding them around the shank in close connecting spirals to your thread near the eye of the hook. Remember to stroke the fibers rearward as you make each turn of doubled hackle around the shank.

7. When you come close to the butt ends of the double hackle you should be fairly close to the eye of the hook. You'll also be getting into the webbier and fluffy fibers near the base of each hackle. Take one or two turns of webbed and fluffy hackle around the shank also. Bring your thread over the shank and secure the hackle. Trim the excess and whip finish.

If your hackle was not long enough to reach the eye of the hook used, by all means add another double-folded unit of hackle and splice it in.

When you get used to tying the Featherduster in this manner you may wish to try your luck and see if you can fold both hackles simultaneously. In other words, don't fold the saddle-hackle feathers separately and insert one into the other, but line up both hackles so that their center stems are against each other and fold both at the same time. Wet your fingers first—it will help.

When this fly is used for fishing Atlantic salmon it is not weighted with lead wire because most of the prime water for Atlantic salmon is in Canada where weighting the fly is not permitted. When fished for trout, a base of fine lead wire helps the fly sink if it is to be fished subsurface as a streamer. (In fishing for salmon it is used as a wet fly that skitters half in and half above the surface film.)

The Salmon (or Trout) Featherduster is also tied using brown-and-grizzly saddle hackle and black-and-orange saddle hackle.

Spider Variant (sizes 16 and 18)
Hook: Mustad 94842, Partridge L3B
Thread: black
Tail: white-to-cream hackle fibers
Underbody: black dubbing fur
Body: full-herled peacock herl
Hackle: oversized white to cream

Spiders or variants generally have an all-hackle makeup, with the exception, in some cases, of a segmented rooster-stem quill body terminating at the hackle collar. With this pattern I have tried to create the illusion of a substantial thorax by adding bulk in that area. The natural spider seems to be all legs but it does have a pronounced body from which these legs protrude. In the Spider Variant we are suspending that body from the end of long legs (hackle) by building up an underbody of black fur and covering that with long-fibered peacock herl before winding the oversized saddle hackle to form the collar. Natural badger hackle also creates a similar illusion but does not quite match the degree of depth and substance or the pulsing, lifelike appearance of the iridescent peacock herl. Tying procedures are relatively simple.

1. Place a size 16 hook in your vise and spiral your thread onto the shank beginning behind the eye and winding to the bend.

2. Tie in a tail of white or cream hackle fibers.

3. Tie in a white-to-cream saddle hackle. Hackle should measure a normal size 8 or 6.

4. Tie in a full and long-fibered section of peacock herl.

5. Spin some black fur onto the thread and form a slightly humped body beginning one-third of the hook shank length forward of the bend, and winding to the eye. Use enough fur so there is a pronounced buildup and so the following herl and hackle will have something to bite into. Since we will be using only one large saddle hackle, the fur underbody will assist in keeping the hackle fibers erect without leaning.

6. Wind the peacock herl through the black fur in connecting spirals in such a manner that the herl fibers stand erect and are not overly bound down.

7. Wind the saddle hackle through the peacock herl for approximately five turns. Trim the excess and whip finish.

The Spider Variant is also tied in natural colors of dun, grizzly, black, and brown as far as the use of the tail and hackle collar are concerned. The body area of black fur and peacock herl remains the same.

Spruce Creek Fly (sizes 16–18)
Hook: Mustad 94840

Thread: black
Wing: wood-duck flank fibers (upright divided), or mottled tan/brown hen saddle fibers
Tail: black hackle fibers
Body: stripped peacock-sword quill
Hackle: black or iron dun

The foregoing pattern, designed by George Harvey, has proven a highly effective pattern in a relatively short period of time. Take note that the body is made from one of the very long stripped peacock sword fibers that grow from the lower portion of the quill. This quill is very dark and has no segmentation. Tying procedures for this pattern are the same as those for any conventional dry fly.

Spider Variant

Tail, hackle, and peacock herl have been tied to shank.

Dubbing being wound around shank.

Peacock herl has been wound over dubbing.

Hackle has been wound through peacock herl to complete fly. Note dark area of peacock herl showing through white fibers.

If, when you close the pages of this book, you have learned or discovered a new method or technique, or found a better way in certain procedures to use various types of hackle, then my time has been well spent. I urge you to experiment on your own with the use of hackles and the creation of new flies. That, after all, is what fly tying is all about.

Good tying and good fishing.

Index

(Note: Page numbers in italics refer to illustrations)